LANGUAGE!®

The Comprehensive Literacy Curriculum

Jane Fell Greene, Ed.D.

Sopris West®
EDUCATIONAL SERVICES

A Cambium Learning® Company

BOSTON, MA · LONGMONT, CO

5 6 7   HPS   14 13 12 11

Authors:
Jane Fell Greene, Ed.D.
Nancy Chapel Eberhardt

ISBN 13 digit: 978-1-60218-698-9
ISBN 10 digit: 1-60218-698-7

170042/3-11

Printed in the United States of America

Published and distributed by

Sopris West®
EDUCATIONAL SERVICES

A Cambium Learning® Company

4093 Specialty Place • Longmont, CO 80504 • (303) 651-2829
www.sopriswest.com

Table of Contents

Check off the activities you complete with each lesson. Evaluate your accomplishments at the end of each lesson. Pay attention to teacher evaluations and comments.

Unit Objectives (Lessons 1-5)	Lesson 1 (Date:_____)	Lesson 2 (Date:_____)
STEP 1 • Identify closed syllables. • Identify stressed and unstressed syllables in multisyllable words.	❑ Review: Vowels ❑ Review: Consonants ❑ Syllable Awareness: Segmentation	❑ Syllable Awareness: Segmentation ❑ Review: Closed Syllables ❑ Exercise 1: Listening for Sounds in Words
STEP 2 • Spell words composed of closed syllables. • Read fluently and spelll the **Essential Words:** *gone, look, most, people, see, water.* • Read fluently words composed of closed syllables and words with prefixes **dis-, in-, non-, un-.**	❑ Exercise 1: Spelling Pretest 1 ❑ Memorize It	❑ Review: Syllables ❑ Exercise 2: Listening for Word Parts ❑ Exercise 3: Build It ❑ Word Fluency 1 ❑ Memorize It: Essential Words ❑ Handwriting Practice
STEP 3 • Identify synonyms, antonyms, homophones, and attributes for **Unit Words.** • Identiy the meaning of prefixes in words	❑ Explore It ❑ Expression of the Day	❑ Review: Compound Words ❑ Exercise 4: Sort It: Compound Words ❑ Compound Words: Three Kinds ❑ Exercise 5: Find It: Compound Words ❑ Expression of the Day
STEP 4 • Identify and use **be** as a helping verb. • Identify the noun or pronoun as subject.	❑ Review: Nouns ❑ Exercise 2: Identify It: Nouns ❑ Review: Pronouns ❑ Exercise 3: Find It: Pronouns	❑ Review: Verbs Using the Tense Timeline ❑ Exercise 6: Identify It: Past, Present, and Future
STEP 5 • Read phrases and passages fluently. • Define vocabulary using context-based strategies or a reference source. • Preview reading selection using text features. • Identify factual information by listening to and reading informational text.	❑ Exercise 4: Phrase It ❑ Independent Text: "Off-the-Wall Inventions" ❑ Exercise 5: Find It: Closed Syllables	❑ Passage Fluency 1 ❑ Exercise 7: Use the Clues: Vocabulary Strategies
STEP 6 • Generate sentences using a six-stage process. • Answer comprehension questions beginning with **use, generalize, infer, illustrate,** and **explain.** • Write an expository paragraph. • Identify and write parts of an expository report including introductory paragraph, transition topic sentence, E's, and concluding paragraph.	❑ Masterpiece Sentences: Stages 1–4	❑ Summarize It
Self-Evaluation (5 is the highest) **Effort** = I produced my best work. **Participation** = I was actively involved in tasks. **Independence** = I worked on my own.	**Effort:** 1 2 3 4 5 **Participation:** 1 2 3 4 5 **Independence:** 1 2 3 4 5	**Effort:** 1 2 3 4 5 **Participation:** 1 2 3 4 5 **Independence:** 1 2 3 4 5
Teacher Evaluation	**Effort:** 1 2 3 4 5 **Participation:** 1 2 3 4 5 **Independence:** 1 2 3 4 5	**Effort:** 1 2 3 4 5 **Participation:** 1 2 3 4 5 **Independence:** 1 2 3 4 5

Lesson 3 (Date:_____)	Lesson 4 (Date:_____)	Lesson 5 (Date:_____)
❑ Syllable Awareness: Segmentation ❑ Exercise 1: Listening for Sounds in Words	❑ Exercise 1: Syllable Awareness: Segmentation	❑ Content Mastery: Syllable Awareness
❑ Review: Closed Syllables ❑ Exercise 2: Find It: Essential Words ❑ Word Fluency 1	❑ Introduce: Prefixes ❑ Exercise 2: Find It: Prefixes ❑ Exercise 3: Sort It: Prefixes ❑ Word Fluency 2 ❑ Type It	❑ Content Mastery: Spelling Posttest 1
❑ Exercise 3: Define It ❑ Draw It: Idioms ❑ Expression of the Day	❑ Review: Prefixes ❑ Exercise 4: Match It: Using Prefixes ❑ Expression of the Day	❑ Review: Antonyms, Synonyms, and Attributes ❑ Exercise 1: Word Relationships: Antonyms, Synonyms, and Attributes ❑ Draw It: Idioms ❑ Expression of the Day
❑ Review: The Verb *Be* ❑ Exercise 4: Identify It: *Be*–Main Verb or Helping Verb ❑ Exercise 5: Identify It: The Verb *Be*	❑ Exercise 5: Tense Timeline	❑ Review: Subject and Predicate ❑ Masterpiece Sentences: Stages 1–3 ❑ Masterpiece Sentences: Helping Verbs
❑ Instructional Text: "It'll Never Work" Exercise 6: Use the Clues: Vocabulary Strategies	❑ Report Structure	❑ Prepare to Write: Multiparagraph Report
❑ Exercise 7: Answer It: Using Signal Words	❑ Review: Write an Expository Paragraph Exercise 6: Write It: Expository Paragraph	❑ Review: Two-Sentence Introductory Paragraph Exercise 2: Write It: Two-Sentence Introduction
Effort: 1 2 3 4 5 **Participation:** 1 2 3 4 5 **Independence:** 1 2 3 4 5	**Effort:** 1 2 3 4 5 **Participation:** 1 2 3 4 5 **Independence:** 1 2 3 4 5	**Effort:** 1 2 3 4 5 **Participation:** 1 2 3 4 5 **Independence:** 1 2 3 4 5
Effort: 1 2 3 4 5 **Participation:** 1 2 3 4 5 **Independence:** 1 2 3 4 5	**Effort:** 1 2 3 4 5 **Participation:** 1 2 3 4 5 **Independence:** 1 2 3 4 5	**Effort:** 1 2 3 4 5 **Participation:** 1 2 3 4 5 **Independence:** 1 2 3 4 5

Check off the activities you complete with each lesson. Evaluate your accomplishments at the end of each lesson. Pay attention to teacher evaluations and comments.

Unit Objectives (Lessons 6-10)	Lesson 6 (Date:_____)	Lesson 7 (Date:_____)
STEP 1 • Identify stressed and unstressed syllables in multisyllable words. • Recognize the schwa in multisyllable words	❑ Exercise 1: Listening for Stressed Syllables	❑ Introduce: Shifting the Syllable Stress ❑ Exercise 1: Listening for Stressed Syllables ❑ Introduce: Schwa ❑ Schwa in the Unstressed Syllable
STEP 2 • Spell words composed of closed syllables. • Read fluently and spell words composed of closed syllables and words with prefixes **dis-, in-, non-, un-**. • Read fluently and spell the **Essential Words**: *gone, look, most, people, see, water*. • Read and spell contractions with **am** and **is**.	❑ Exercise 2: Spelling Pretest 2 ❑ Word Fluency 3	❑ Build It: Words with Schwa ❑ Review: Contractions ❑ Exercise 2: Contract It ❑ Review: Its and It's ❑ Exercise 3: Choose It and Use It
STEP 3 • Identify synonyms, antonyms, homophones, and attributes for **Unit Words**. • Identify the meaning of prefixes in words	❑ Exercise 3: Word Relationships: Antonyms, Synonyms, and Attributes ❑ Expression of the Day	❑ Review: Prefixes ❑ Exercise 4: Match It: Using Prefixes ❑ Expression of the Day
STEP 4 • Identify and use **be** as a helping verb. • Identify the noun or pronoun as subject. • Identify direct objects.	❑ Review: Simple Subject and Simple Predicate ❑ Review: Direct Objects ❑ Exercise 4: Code It: Direct Object	❑ Shifting Syllable Stress: Grammatical Implications ❑ Exercise 5: Code It: Noun or Verb
STEP 5 • Read phrases and passages fluently. • Define vocabulary using context-based strategies or a reference source. • Preview reading selection using text features. • Identify factual information by listening to and reading informational text.	❑ Exercise 5: Phrase It ❑ Independent Text: **"Solving Problems"** Exercise 6: Use the Clues: Vocabulary Strategies	❑ Passage Fluency 2 ❑ Exercise 6: Use the Clues: Vocabulary Strategies
STEP 6 • Answer comprehension questions beginning with **use, generalize, infer, illustrate,** and **explain**. • Record information in an informal (two-column) outline. • Identify and write parts of an expository report including introductory paragraph, transition topic sentence, E's, and concluding paragraph. • Write an expository report..	❑ Exercise 7: Rewrite It	❑ Report Structure Exercise 7: Write It: Transition Topic Sentence

Self-Evaluation (5 is the highest)	Effort: 1 2 3 4 5	Effort: 1 2 3 4 5
Effort = I produced my best work. **Participation** = I was actively involved in tasks. **Independence** = I worked on my own.	Participation: 1 2 3 4 5 Independence: 1 2 3 4 5	Participation: 1 2 3 4 5 Independence: 1 2 3 4 5
Teacher Evaluation	Effort: 1 2 3 4 5 Participation: 1 2 3 4 5 Independence: 1 2 3 4 5	Effort: 1 2 3 4 5 Participation: 1 2 3 4 5 Independence: 1 2 3 4 5

Lesson 8 (Date:_____)	Lesson 9 (Date:_____)	Lesson 10 (Date:_____)
❑ Review: Stressed Syllables ❑ Exercise 1: Listening for Stressed Syllables ❑ Review: Schwa ❑ Vowel Chart	❑ Review: Stressed Syllables ❑ Review: Shifting the Syllable Stress ❑ Exercise 1: Listening for Stressed Syllables	❑ Exercise 1: Listening for Stressed Syllables
❑ Divide It ❑ Word Fluency 4	❑ Exercise 2: Build It	❑ Content Mastery: Spelling Posttest 2
❑ Content Mastery: Word Relationships; Prefixes	❑ Exercise 3: Find It: Compound Words and Words with Prefixes ❑ Exercise 4: Sort It: Compound Words and Words with Prefixes ❑ Exercise 5: Define It ❑ Expression of the Day	❑ Explore It: Inventions ❑ Draw It: Idioms ❑ Expression of the Day
❑ Diagram It ❑ Exercise 2: Diagram It: Subject, Verb, and Direct Object	❑ Masterpiece Sentences: Stages 1 and 2	❑ Content Mastery: Helping Verbs; Nouns or Pronouns; Nouns and Pronouns as Direct Objects
❑ Instructional Text: "Way to Go!" ❑ Exercise 3: Use the Clues: Vocabulary Strategies	❑ Prepare to Write: Expository Report	❑ Write It: Expository Report
❑ Exercise 4: Answer It: Using Signal Words	❑ Organize Information: Informal Outline Exercise 6: Create an Informal Outline for a Report	❑ Check It: Draft of an Expository Report
Effort: 1 2 3 4 5 **Participation:** 1 2 3 4 5 **Independence:** 1 2 3 4 5	**Effort:** 1 2 3 4 5 **Participation:** 1 2 3 4 5 **Independence:** 1 2 3 4 5	**Effort:** 1 2 3 4 5 **Participation:** 1 2 3 4 5 **Independence:** 1 2 3 4 5
Effort: 1 2 3 4 5 **Participation:** 1 2 3 4 5 **Independence:** 1 2 3 4 5	**Effort:** 1 2 3 4 5 **Participation:** 1 2 3 4 5 **Independence:** 1 2 3 4 5	**Effort:** 1 2 3 4 5 **Participation:** 1 2 3 4 5 **Independence:** 1 2 3 4 5

Exercise 1 · Spelling Pretest 1

▸ Write each word your teacher repeats.

1. _____   6. _____   11. _____

2. _____   7. _____   12. _____

3. _____   8. _____   13. _____

4. _____   9. _____   14. _____

5. _____   10. _____   15. _____

Exercise 2 · Identify It: Nouns

▸ Read the excerpt from **"Off-the-Wall Inventions"** below.

▸ Decide if each underlined noun names a person, place, thing, or idea.

▸ Write the noun in the correct column in the chart below.

▸ Do the first one with your teacher. **Hint:** One of the words can be in two columns.

---

based on "Off-the-Wall Inventions"

Drive the C5

Step back in time. It is 1985. In **England**, a man makes a **bike** with
$_1$ $_2$
3 wheels. This bike is not ridden. It's driven! C5 is its name. The
C5 has an upside; it runs on **batteries**, not gas! It does not emit gas
$_3$
fumes. Ships use C5s. The small C5s can drive across the **decks** of
$_4$
big ships. A C5 helps move things on a ship, but it has a downside.
If you drive the C5 in **traffic**, you will find that it's too small and
$_5$
sluggish. Also, the **driver** is exposed. Passing cars emit gas fumes.
$_6$
The driver inhales these toxic fumes! This is quite a **problem**. Back
$_7$
to the present. There is a contest for **students**. Students make odd
$_8$
things. The oddest invention wins. Do you have an "off-the-wall"
plan? Invent something that makes us smile, and you might win a
$_9$
trip to **Mars**, on a C5!
$_{10}$

Persons	Places	Things	Ideas

Exercise 3 · Find It: Pronouns

▸ Read each sentence.

▸ Underline the pronoun.

▸ Fill in the bubble to show whether the pronoun is a subject pronoun or an object pronoun.

▸ Do the first one with your teacher.

	subject	object
1. We were helping Jan.	◯	◯
2. She was expanding the report.	◯	◯
3. Jane was expanding it.	◯	◯
4. We connected the dots.	◯	◯
5. The inventions amazed them.	◯	◯

Exercise 4 · Phrase It

▶ Use a pencil to "scoop" the phrases in each sentence.

▶ Then read each sentence as you would say it.

▶ The first sentence is done for you.

1. Some inventors create devices just for fun.

2. They are "off-the-wall."

3. They will not have an impact.

4. A fad is a quick craze.

5. He had invented lots of nutty things.

6. He just loves tinkering.

7. Step back in time to 1985.

8. The C5 runs on batteries, not gas.

9. It emits no gas fumes.

10. A C5 helps move things on a ship.

Unit 13 · Lesson 1

Exercise 5 · Find It: Closed Syllables

▸ Listen to your teacher read the text.

▸ Reread the text silently or quietly to yourself.

▸ Highlight **closed syllables** with short vowels in words.

▸ Sort each closed syllable according to its short vowel sound.

▸ Record nonphonetic words and words that you're unsure of in the last column under the "**?**"

> **based on "Off-the-Wall Inventions"**
>
> Some inventions were made just for fun. Some of them are odd. Many of them have odd names. They are just not useful. Not many of them will sell. They will not have any impact.

ă	ĕ	ĭ	ŏ	ŭ	?

Exercise 1 · Listening for Sounds in Words

▸ Listen to each word your teacher says.

▸ Identify the short vowel sound.

▸ Mark the short vowel sound with a breve (˘).

1. a   e   i   o   u
2. a   e   i   o   u
3. a   e   i   o   u
4. a   e   i   o   u
5. a   e   i   o   u
6. a   e   i   o   u
7. a   e   i   o   u
8. a   e   i   o   u
9. a   e   i   o   u
10. a   e   i   o   u

Unit 13 · Lesson 2

Exercise 2 · Listening for Word Parts

▸ Listen to each word your teacher says.

▸ Write the word part that your teacher repeats.

1. _____   2. _____   3. _____   4. _____   5. _____

6. _____   7. _____   8. _____   9. _____   10. _____

Exercise 3 · Build It

▸ Use the answers from Exercise 2, **Listening for Word Parts**.

▸ Combine word parts to create new words.

_____   _____   _____

_____   _____   _____

▸ Circle the compound words.

▸ Answer this question:

How do you know the words that you circled are compound words?

_____

_____

Exercise 4 · Sort It: Compound Words

▶ Decide whether the parts of each compound help with the meaning.

▶ Write the word in the correct column.

▶ The first two are done for you.

Compound Word	Last Part Names the Item	Not the Sum of the Parts
Example: downhill	downhill	
Example: laptop		laptop
1. windfall		
2. fishnet		
3. clamshell		
4. hotshot		
5. spyglass		
6. smalltime		
7. upscale		
8. gemstone		
9. makeshift		
10. dishcloth		

Exercise 5 · Find It: Compound Words

▸ Use your dictionary to find compound words with **jump** and compound words with **back**.

▸ Write each word in the correct column.

Connected (Closed)	Hyphenated	Spaced Apart (Open)
Example: jumpsuit	**Example:** jump-start	**Example:** jump shot

Exercise 6 · Identify It: Past, Present, and Future

▶ Decide whether the underlined verb or verb phrase shows action in the past, present, or future.

▶ Fill in the correct bubble.

▶ Do the first one with your teacher.

	Past	Present	Future
1. They <u>will adapt</u> to their new school.	◯	◯	◯
2. He <u>assisted</u> the small children at the bus stop.	◯	◯	◯
3. I <u>am attaching</u> this lock to my bike.	◯	◯	◯
4. They <u>collect</u> dozens of jackets for people.	◯	◯	◯
5. Our campus <u>expanded</u> by more than 100 students this month.	◯	◯	◯
6. They <u>will suspend</u> bids on that project.	◯	◯	◯
7. We <u>are finishing</u> our project this month.	◯	◯	◯
8. They <u>will be selecting</u> a president this fall.	◯	◯	◯
9. His lunch <u>vanished</u> in about six seconds.	◯	◯	◯
10. We <u>are visiting</u> our granddad at his cabin.	◯	◯	◯

Unit 13 · Lesson 2

Exercise 7 · Use the Clues: Vocabulary Strategies

▸ Read the sentence pairs.

▸ Circle the pronoun in the second sentence.

▸ Identify the noun that the pronoun is replacing in each sentence.

▸ Draw an arrow to show the link between the pronoun and the noun it replaced.

▸ Underline the noun that the pronoun is referring to.

1. Some inventions are made just for fun. Many of them have odd names.

2. Fads become the rage. People like them.

3. Meet Mr. Robinson. He has invented lots of nutty things.

4. In England, a man is making a small 3-wheeled bike. It is called the C5.

5. If you drive a C5 in traffic, you'll find that it is too small. It's too sluggish.

Exercise 1 · Listening for Sounds in Words

▸ Listen for the short vowel sound in each word your teacher says.

▸ Write the letter for the vowel sound in the position where you hear it.

▸ Mark the vowel with a breve (ĕ) to show the sound.

1. [| |]

2. [| |]

3. [| |]

4. [| |]

5. [| | |]

6. [| |]

7. [| |]

8. [| | |]

9. [| |]

10. [| | |]

Unit 13 · Lesson 3

Exercise 2 · Find It: Essential Words

▶ Write the **Essential Words** on the lines.

_____   _____   _____   _____   _____   _____

▶ Write the sentences that your teacher dictates.

1. _____

2. _____

3. _____

4. _____

▶ Find the six **Essential Words** for this unit in the dictated sentences.

▶ Underline them. There may be more than one in a sentence.

Exercise 3 · Define It

▶ Fill in the blanks with a category and an attribute to define the word.

▶ If you're unsure of your definition, compare it with the word's definition in a dictionary.

▶ Do the first two words with your teacher.

1. An **atlas** is _____ that _____
                  category   **attribute(s)**
   _____.

2. A **clamshell** is _____ that _____
                  category   **attribute(s)**
   _____.

3. A **fishnet** is _____ that _____
   _____.

(continued)

Exercise 3 (continued) · Define It

4. A **laptop** is _____ that _____

   _____.

5. A **jacket** is _____ that _____

   _____.

6. **Cotton** is _____ that _____

   _____.

7. A **magnet** is _____ that _____

   _____.

8. A **checklist** is _____ that _____

   _____.

9. A **ticket** is _____ that _____

   _____

   _____.

10. **Water** is _____ that _____

   _____

   _____.

▶ Which words in bold type are compound words?

▶ Write the compound words on the lines.

_____ _____ _____ _____

Unit 13 · Lesson 3

Exercise 4 · Identify It: *Be*—Main Verb or Helping Verb

PERSON	Past		Present		Future	
	singular	plural	singular	plural	singular	plural
1st person	*(I)* was	*(we)* were	*(I)* am	*(we)* are	*(I)* will be	*(we)* will be
2nd person	*(you)* were	*(you)* were	*(you)* are	*(you)* are	*(you)* will be	*(you)* will be
3rd person	*(he, she, it)* was	*(they)* were	*(he, she, it)* is	*(they)* are	*(he, she, it)* will be	*(they)* will be

▸ Identify the form of the verb **be** in each of the following sentences. Use the chart to help you.

▸ Underline the form of **be**.

▸ Fill in the bubble to show if the form of **be** is used as a main verb or a helping verb.

	Main Verb	Helping Verb
1. We are inventors.	◯	◯
2. She was writing a report.	◯	◯
3. He will be president of his class.	◯	◯
4. You were listening to a famous song.	◯	◯
5. I am collecting cans for my project.	◯	◯

Exercise 5 · Identify It: The Verb *Be*

▸ Use the chart in Exercise 4 to identify the helping verbs (forms of **be**) in these sentences.

▸ Circle the helping verb or verbs.

▸ Fill in the bubble after each sentence to show if the verb is in the past, present, or future tense.

	Past	Present	Future
1. We will be collecting shells.	◯	◯	◯
2. She was expanding her report.	◯	◯	◯
3. He is connecting the segments.	◯	◯	◯
4. They were selecting the ones they liked.	◯	◯	◯
5. I am finishing the project today.	◯	◯	◯

Unit 13 · Lesson 3

Exercise 6 · Use the Clues: Vocabulary Strategies

1. Work along with your teacher to use meaning cues to define **tricycle**.

   The Sinclair C5 vehicle was a tricycle, which means it had three wheels.

2. Use meaning cues to define **multipurpose**.
   - Underline the vocabulary word.
   - Read the sentence aloud and look for a meaning cue.
   - Circle the meaning cue words.
   - Double underline the words that define **multipurpose**.
   - Draw an arrow from the underlined word to the definition.

   > **based on "It'll Never Work"**
   >
   > A second unsuccessful invention was a multipurpose machine, which means it had many functions. One invention tried to be everything. It was a car. It was a boat. It was a plane. It was all three. Too bad the idea didn't take off. And neither did the machine.

3. Define the word **multipurpose** in your own words.

   _____

   _____

   _____

4. Verify your definition of **multipurpose** by using a dictionary reference source.

Exercise 7 · Answer It: Using Signal Words

▸ Underline the signal word in each question.

▸ Write the answer in a complete sentence or sentences.

▸ Check for sentence signals—capital letters and end punctuation.

1. Choose one of the inventions from **"It'll Never Work."** Infer something about its inventor.

   _____

   _____

   _____

2. What can you generalize about the types of inventions described in the section of text titled "Some Inventions That Never Took Off"?

   _____

   _____

   _____

3. Illustrate one of the inventions in the section of text titled "Strange But True: Other Unbelievable Inventions."

   ┌───┐
   │   │
   │   │
   │   │
   │   │
   │   │
   │   │
   └───┘

(continued)

Exercise 7 *(continued)* · **Answer It: Using Signal Words**

4. What can you infer about the reason inventors created products in the section "Strange But True"?

_____

_____

_____

5. What can you infer about who Rube Goldberg was from the last paragraph of this selection?

_____

_____

_____

Exercise 1 · Syllable Awareness: Segmentation

▸ Listen to each word your teacher says.

▸ Count the syllables. Write the number in the first column.

▸ Write the letter for each vowel sound you hear.

▸ Mark each short vowel with a breve (˘).

	How many syllables do you hear?	First vowel sound	Second vowel sound
1.			
2.			
3.			
4.			
5.			
6.			
7.			
8.			
9.			
10.			

Unit 13 · Lesson 4

Exercise 2 · Find It: Prefixes

▸ Circle the prefix, **dis-**, **in-**, **un-**, or **non-**, in each word below.

▸ Blend the prefix and the base word to read the entire word.

nonfat	unclasp	inland	distrust
nonskid	disarm	input	unbent
distract	nonstick	nonstop	unplug
instep	unfit	unlock	inside

Exercise 3 · Sort It: Prefixes

▸ Sort the words from Exercise 2, **Find It: Prefixes**, by prefix. Write each word in the correct column in the chart.

▸ One example of each prefix is done for you.

▸ Read the words to a partner.

dis-	in-	non-	un-
distrust	inland	nonfat	unclasp

Exercise 4 · Match It: Using Prefixes

▶ Draw a line to match each word or prefix with its definition. Use what you know about the prefix **un-** to help you.

▶ Use a dictionary for help if necessary.

Word/Prefix	Definition
1. unwell	**a.** to undo a button
2. unfit	**b.** take out of a container, undo the packing
3. unpack	**c.** not, opposite
4. unbutton	**d.** not well, unhealthy, sick.
5. un-	**e.** not fit, weak

▶ Look at definitions for items 1–5. What words do they have in common?

_____

▶ Draw a line to match each word or prefix with its definition. Use what you know about the prefix **non-** to help you.

▶ Use a dictionary for help if necessary.

Word/Prefix	Definition
6. nonstop	**a.** without sense, foolishness
7. nonsense	**b.** not equal
8. nontoxic	**c.** without stop, made or done without stop or stopping
9. non-equal	**d.** without, not or no
10. non-	**e.** without or not toxic, without poison(s)

▶ Look at definitions for items 6–10. What words do they have in common?

_____

Unit 13 · Lesson 4

Exercise 5 · Tense Timeline

▸ Read the five sentences below.

▸ Write the verb or verb phrase in the correct position on the **Tense Timeline**.

▸ Expand the verb to include six total forms: *past, present, future, past progressive, present progressive,* and *future progressive.*

1. I **punished** my dog for digging up the garden.

Past	Present	Future

2. We **will be visiting** the museum with the other classes.

3. He **was admitting** his problem.

4. Time **is vanishing**.

5. She **connects** them with others.

Exercise 6 · Write It: Expository Paragraph

▶ Read the prompt below. Underline the signal word and circle the topic.

▶ Use the following prompt and outline as a guide to write an expository paragraph.

Prompt: Describe how inventions solve problems.

Informal Outline	
Topic = Inventions solve problems	
★ New methods	— Plastic for cars
★ New uses	— Recycle plastic bottles

Conclusion = Inventions can help us

_____

_____

_____

_____

_____

_____

_____

Exercise 1 • Word Relationships: Antonyms, Synonyms, and Attributes

Antonyms

▶ Read the words in the **Word Bank**.

Word Bank

under	top	uncommon
connect	simple	across

▶ Select and write the antonym (opposite) for each word your teacher says.

▶ Discuss your answers.

1. bottom _____   **4.** complex _____

2. disconnect _____   **5.** common _____

3. over _____

Synonyms

▶ Read the words in the **Word Bank**.

Word Bank

bottom	finish	vanish
observe	uncommon	nonstop

▶ Select and write the synonym (same or almost the same) for each word your teacher says.

▶ Discuss your answers.

6. base _____   **9.** watch _____

7. end _____   **10.** disappear _____

8. direct _____

(continued)

Exercise 1 (continued) · Word Relationships: Antonyms, Synonyms, and Attributes

Attributes

▸ Read the words in the **Word Bank**.

Word Bank

white	buttons	bottom
dozen	facts	thin

▸ Select and write the attribute (size, part, color, function) for each word your teacher says.

▸ Discuss your answers.

11. textbook _____

12. snow _____

13. jacket _____

14. ribbon _____

15. eggs _____

Exercise 2 · Write It: Two-Sentence Introduction

▸ Read each prompt and circle the signal word.

▸ Underline the topic and write it in the space provided.

▸ Brainstorm possible "star ideas" for the topic. Write them next to the stars.

▸ Write a sentence that states the topic.

▸ Write a plan sentence based on the topic sentence.

▸ Write the topic sentence and plan sentence together to finish the two-sentence introduction.

1. **Prompt:** Describe your pets, or pets you'd like to have.

    Topic: _____

    ★ _____

    ★ _____

    ★ _____

    State the Topic: _____

    _____

    State the Plan: _____

    _____

    _____

    Two-Sentence Introductory Paragraph: _____

    _____

    _____

    _____

    _____

(continued)

Exercise 2 (continued) · Write It: Two-Sentence Introduction

2. **Prompt**: Describe two or three of your favorite bands or musicians.

Topic: _____

★ _____

★ _____

★ _____

State the Topic: _____

_____

State the Plan: _____

_____

_____

Two-Sentence Introductory Paragraph: _____

_____

_____

_____

_____

(continued)

Exercise 2 (continued) · Write It: Two-Sentence Introduction

3. **Prompt:** Tell where you would go and what you would do if you could visit a foreign country.

Topic: _____

★ _____

★ _____

★ _____

State the Topic: _____

_____

State the Plan: _____

_____

_____

Two-Sentence Introductory Paragraph: _____

_____

_____

_____

_____

(continued)

Exercise 2 (continued) · Write It: Two-Sentence Introduction

4. **Prompt**: Describe some easy ways students can get more exercise.

Topic: _____

★ _____

★ _____

★ _____

State the Topic: _____

_____

State the Plan: _____

_____

_____

Two-Sentence Introductory Paragraph: _____

_____

_____

_____

_____

Exercise 1 · Listening for Stressed Syllables

▸ Listen to the word your teacher says.

▸ Repeat the word.

▸ Listen for the stressed syllable.

▸ Make an X in the box to mark the position of the stressed syllable.

	1st Syllable	2nd Syllable
Example: pilgrim	X	
1. inflict		
2. magnet		
3. camel		
4. adapt		
5. method		

Exercise 2 · Spelling Pretest 2

▸ Listen to the word your teacher repeats.

▸ Write the word.

1. _____   6. _____   11. _____

2. _____   7. _____   12. _____

3. _____   8. _____   13. _____

4. _____   9. _____   14. _____

5. _____   10. _____   15. _____

Unit 13 · Lesson 6

Exercise 3 · Word Relationships: Antonyms, Synonyms, and Attributes

▸ Read each pair of words.

▸ Sort word pairs according to their relationship. Write the word pairs in the correct column.

▸ Discuss answers with your partner.

base : bottom	bottom : top	jacket : buttons	disconnect : connect
ribbon : thin	end : finish	common : uncommon	disappear : vanish
over : above	eggs : dozen	cotton : soft	nonstop : stop

Antonyms (Opposite)	Synonyms (Same)	Attributes

Exercise 4 · Code It: Direct Object

▸ Draw one line under the simple subject. Code it **SS**.

▸ Draw two lines under the simple predicate. Code it **SP**.

▸ Find the direct object. Code it **DO**.

1. The timid old man sipped the hot broth.

2. His plastic flute made a distinct tune.

3. The class constructed a huge rocket for the contest.

4. The invention used a hundred magnets.

5. The intense inventor examined her complex plans.

Exercise 5 · Phrase It

▸ Use a pencil to "scoop" the phrases in each sentence.

▸ Then read each sentence as you would say it.

▸ The first two sentences are done for you.

1. Inventors have quick minds.

2. They think about problems.

3. Inventors begin with a problem.

4. Cars use too much gas.

5. The gas makes fumes.

6. Make a car of plastic.

7. It would use less gas.

8. Plastic lasts a long time.

9. Less plastic would go into landfills.

10. We would help save our planet.

Exercise 6 · Use the Clues: Vocabulary Strategies

▶ Read each pair of sentences.

▶ Find the pronoun that is circled.

▶ Underline the noun that the pronoun replaces.

▶ Draw an arrow to show the link between the pronoun and the noun it replaced.

1. Inventors have quick minds. (They) think about problems.

2. Inventions impact our lives. (They) make our lives better.

3. A patent confirms your ownership. (It) means that your invention belongs to you.

4. Inventors begin with a problem. They think about (it.)

5. Inventors begin with a problem. This is how (they) think.

Exercise 7 · Rewrite It

▶ Read each sentence pair in Exercise 6, **Use the Clues: Vocabulary Strategies**.

▶ Replace the circled pronoun with the noun that it represents.

▶ Rewrite the sentence using the noun.

▶ Check for sentence signals—capital letters, commas, and end punctuation.

▶ Read the new sentence.

1. _____

2. _____

3. _____

4. _____

5. _____

Exercise 1 · Listening for Stressed Syllables

▸ Listen to each word and sentence your teacher says.

▸ Repeat the word.

▸ Listen for the stressed, or accented, syllable.

▸ Put an X in the box to mark the position of the stressed syllable.

▸ Do the first two with your teacher.

1. ☒ ☐

2. ☐ ☒

3. ☐ ☐

4. ☐ ☐

5. ☐ ☐

6. ☐ ☐

7. ☐ ☐

8. ☐ ☐

9. ☐ ☐

10. ☐ ☐

Exercise 2 · Contract It

▶ Read each sentence.

▶ Circle the contraction.

▶ Write the contraction and the two words that make up the contracted form.

▶ The first one is done for you.

1. (I'm) about to disrupt the suspect.

2. It's too late to submit your chart.

3. He's investing his money in nonfat dressings.

4. It's uncommon to see foxes on campus.

5. She's ticketing him for littering in the park.

1. I'm = I + am

2. _____

3. _____

4. _____

5. _____

Unit 13 · Lesson 7

Exercise 3 · Choose It and Use It

▸ Fill in the blank with **its** or **it's**.
  Hint: It's = it is.

▸ Replace **it's** with **it is**.

▸ Reread the sentence to see if the sentence makes sense.

1. Step back in time. _____ 1985.

2. This bike is not ridden. _____ driven.

3. C5 is _____ name.

4. _____ not as big as a ship.

5. Fabric stretches across _____ frame.

6. _____ downside is speed.

7. _____ not fast because _____ engine is run by batteries.

8. You will find that _____ too small and sluggish to drive in traffic.

9. _____ driver would be exposed to toxic fumes.

10. _____ an "off-the-wall" invention.

Exercise 4 · Match It: Using Prefixes

▶ Draw a line to match each word or prefix to its definition. Use what you know about the prefix **in-** to help you.

▶ Use a dictionary to verify answers.

Word/Prefix	Definition
1. inland	a. to write inside of a book or on a stone
2. income	b. into
3. indent	c. to notch into an edge
4. inscribe	d. located inside of a country, away from the ocean or shore
5. in-	e. money that comes in

▶ Look at definitions for items 1–5. What words do they have in common?

_____.

▶ Draw a line to match each word or prefix to the definition. Use what you know about the prefix **dis-** to help you.

▶ Use a dictionary to verify answers.

Word/Prefix	Definition
6. disprove	a. to not like, the opposite of like
7. disband	b. to move something away from its usual place, often by force
8. dislike	c. to prove wrong; to prove that something is the opposite of truth
9. displace	d. to break up or undo an organization or group (band)
10. dis-	e. apart, away, and sometimes the opposite of

▶ Look at definitions for items 6–10. What words do they have in common?

_____.

Exercise 5 · Code It: Noun or Verb

▸ Read each sentence.

▸ Write **N** if the underlined word is a noun. Write **V** if it is a verb.

▸ The first one is done for you.

      N

1. <u>Conduct</u> is an aspect of your grade.

2. You must <u>conduct</u> the contest by the rules.

3. The <u>object</u> of their plan was escape.

4. I <u>object</u> to the complex plans.

5. Dr. Smith will <u>present</u> the contest rules to the class.

6. His <u>present</u> was an atlas.

7. Will they <u>subject</u> us to a written test?

8. The <u>subject</u> of the test is fractions.

9. His <u>affect</u> was quite odd.

10. His timid manner will <u>affect</u> us.

Exercise 6 · Use the Clues: Vocabulary Strategies

▸ Read the passage.

▸ Reread the underlined sentences with circled pronouns.

▸ Draw an arrow to show the link between the circled pronoun and the noun it replaced in the paragraph.

▸ The first one is done for you.

---

based on "Solving Problems"

Inventors begin with a problem. Most cars use too much gas. Make a car of plastic. That could solve it. The car wouldn't be so heavy. It would use less gas. It would pollute less. Plastic lasts a long time. It doesn't rust. The color doesn't fade. There would be a bonus, too. Think of all the juice we drink. Juice comes in plastic jugs. We could reuse them.

Exercise 7 · Write It: Transition Topic Sentence

First	One	To begin	Initially	First of all
Second	A second	In addition	Then	Also
Third	Another	Finally	After that	Last

Items 1 and 2

▸ Choose transition words from the box and write them at the beginning of the transition topic sentences.

▸ Use correct capitalization.

1. **Introductory Paragraph:** Leonardo da Vinci is most famous as a painter, but he had many jobs in his lifetime. Three of the jobs Leonardo had were architect, weapons designer, and inventor.

   Transition Topic Sentences

   A. _____ of the jobs Leonardo da Vinci did was design buildings as an architect.

   B. _____ way he supported himself was as a weapons designer.

   C. _____ way Leonardo used his talents was as an inventor.

2. **Introductory Paragraph:** Heath Robinson has created many crazy inventions. Three of his inventions are the spaghetti stretcher, a machine that puts square pegs in round holes, and another device that keeps peas from falling off forks.

   Transition Topic Sentences

   A. _____ of Mr. Robinson's silliest inventions is the spaghetti stretcher.

   B. _____ of his inventions is a machine that puts square pegs in round holes.

   C. _____ invention Mr. Robinson is famous for is his device that keeps peas from falling off forks.

(continued)

Exercise 7 (continued) · Write It: Transition Topic Sentence

Items 3–5

▸ For the next items, listen to your teacher for directions about writing transition words and/or transition topic sentences.

▸ Use correct capitalization.

3. **Introductory Paragraph:** There are three fascinating things you might not know about the desert. It is home to many plants and animals, can be very cold, and sometimes gets a lot of rain.

   Transition Topic Sentences

   A. The _____ thing that surprises many people when they first visit a desert is how many plants and animals live there.

   B. A _____ surprising thing about some deserts is how cold they can get, especially at night.

   C. _____

   _____

4. **Introductory Paragraph:** Engineers have several ideas to make dirigibles safer. They can use better fibers for the shell, fill them with helium, and use solar cells for power instead of gasoline.

   Transition Topic Sentences

   A. _____ way to make dirigibles safer is to use better fibers to build their shells.

   B. _____

   _____

   C. _____

   _____

(continued)

Exercise 7 *(continued)* · Write It: Transition Topic Sentence

5. **Introductory Paragraph:** There are three big reasons the Sinclair C5 did not sell very well. It is too slow, the driver is not safe in an accident, and the driver can inhale gas fumes from passing cars.

Transition Topic Sentences

A. _____

_____

_____

B. _____

_____

_____

C. _____

_____

_____

Exercise 1 · Listening for Stressed Syllables

▸ Listen to the word your teacher says.

▸ Repeat the word. Listen for the stressed, or accented, syllable.

▸ Write the stressed syllable in the correct box.

▸ Do the first one with your teacher.

	1st Syllable	2nd Syllable
1.		
2.		
3.		
4.		
5.		
6.		
7.		
8.		
9.		
10.		

Exercise 2 · Diagram It: Subject, Verb, and Direct Object

▸ Read each sentence.

▸ Diagram each sentence in the space below.

▸ Do the first two sentences with your teacher.

    1. The wind gusted.

    2. The wind affected the crops.

    3. Children collected things.

(continued)

Exercise 2 (continued) · **Diagram It: Subject, Verb, and Direct Object**

4. Lemons love sun.

5. The code vanished.

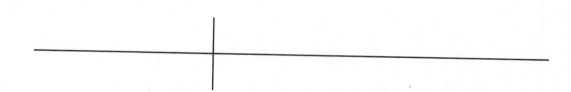

Exercise 3 · Use the Clues: Vocabulary Strategies

1. Work along with your teacher to use meaning cues to define **blimp**.

   A blimp, which is a huge helium balloon, often carries television crews over sporting events.

2. Use meaning cues to define **dirigible**.
   - Underline the word.
   - Read the sentence aloud and look for meaning cue words.
   - Circle each meaning cue word.
   - Double underline the words that define each term.
   - Draw an arrow from the underlined word **dirigible** to its definition.

   based on "Way to Go!"

   A dirigible is sometimes called an airship. Actually, it's a huge helium balloon. Propellers move it. It's similar to a blimp. You've seen blimps on TV. They carry television crews over sports fields. There is a difference between a dirigible and a blimp. A dirigible has a rigid inside frame. This means it can be much bigger than a blimp. A dirigible can carry big loads of cargo and passengers.

3. Define **dirigible** in your own words.

   _____

4. Verify your definitions with either an online dictionary or a print dictionary.

5. List other attributes, or details, about dirigible found in the excerpt.

   _____

   _____

   _____

Exercise 4 · Answer It: Using Signal Words

▸ Underline the signal word in each question.

▸ Write the answers in complete sentences.

▸ Underline the part of your answer that specifically addresses the question.

▸ Check for sentence signals—capital letters and end punctuation.

1. Plastic could be used to produce machines besides cars. Generalize what other types of inventions could be made with recycled plastic.

   _____

   _____

2. Different types of gas have been used to fill dirigibles. What can you infer about the safety of helium as opposed to hydrogen?

   _____

   _____

3. Explain why a person does not need a pilot's license to operate a ground-effect plane.

   _____

   _____

4. What can you generalize about the speed of the inventions in **"Way to Go!"**?

   _____

   _____

5. What can you infer about the impact of new materials on the inventions described in **"Way to Go!"**?

   _____

   _____

   _____

Exercise 1 · Listening for Stressed Syllables

▸ Listen to each word and sentence your teacher says.

▸ Repeat the word. Listen for the stressed, or accented, syllable.

▸ Put an X in the box to mark the position of the stressed syllable.

1. ☐☐

2. ☐☐

3. ☐☐

4. ☐☐

5. ☐☐

6. ☐☐

7. ☐☐

8. ☐☐

9. ☐☐

10. ☐☐

Exercise 2 · Build It

▶ Combine prefixes in the middle square with words and word parts to form new words.

Example: un + plug = unplug.

▶ Record new words in the chart below, according to their prefix.

▶ Use a dictionary to verify that you are building real words.

plug	stick	scribe
connected	in- dis- non- un-	used
-sect	stop	like

non-	un-	in-	dis-

Unit 13 · Lesson 9

Exercise 3 · Find It: Compound Words and Words with Prefixes

▸ Listen to your teacher read the passage.

▸ Reread the passage with a partner.

▸ Find and underline (or highlight) compound words.

▸ Find and underline words with these prefixes: **un-**, **in-**, **dis-**, **non-**.

based on "Way to Go!"

Now That's a Big Balloon!

A dirigible is sometimes called an airship. Actually, it's a huge helium balloon. It may be solar-powered and is a lighter-than-air vehicle. Propellers move it nonstop, through the air over long distances. Dirigibles are similar to the unusual blimps you've seen on TV. Those vehicles carry television crews over sports fields. There is a difference between a dirigible and a blimp. Unlike a blimp, a dirigible has a rigid inside frame. This means it can be much bigger than a blimp. The best-known dirigible was the *Hindenburg*.

Exercise 4 · Sort It: Compound Words and Words with Prefixes

▶ Sort the underlined words from Exercise 3, **Find It: Compound Words and Words with Prefixes**, into the correct columns.

Compound Words	Words with Prefixes

Exercise 5 · Define It

▶ Circle each word below in "Now That's a Big Balloon!" in Exercise 3.

▶ Use context clues and your knowledge of word parts to define each word.

▶ Write the definitions on the lines below.

1. **solar-powered—** _____

_____

2. **nonstop—** _____

_____

3. **unlike—** _____

_____

4. **inside—** _____

_____

5. **best-known—** _____

_____

Exercise 6 · Create an Informal Outline for a Report

▸ Review the informal outline for a single paragraph.

Outline for a Paragraph on the Topic "How Inventions Solve Problems"

Topic = Inventions solve problems

★ New methods	— Plastic for cars
★ New uses	— Recycle plastic bottles

Conclusion = Inventions can help us

▸ Read the informal outline for the report.

▸ Review the elaborations, or E's, in the outline. Add examples and explanations to the blanks in the report outline.

Outline for a Multiparagraph Report on the Topic "How Inventions Solve Problems"

Topic = Inventions solve problems

★ New methods	— Plastic for cars
	• _____
	• _____
	— _____
	• _____
	• _____
★ New uses	— Recycle plastic bottles
	• _____
	• _____
	• _____

Conclusion = Inventions can help us

Exercise 1 · Listening for Stressed Syllables

▸ Listen to each word your teacher says.

▸ Repeat the word and count the syllables. Write the number in the first column.

▸ Write the letter for the vowel sound you hear in each syllable.

▸ Say the word again. Listen for the stressed syllable.

▸ Circle the vowel in the stressed syllable.

	How many syllables do you hear?	First vowel sound	Second vowel sound
1.			
2.			
3.			
4.			
5.			

Check off the activities you complete with each lesson. Evaluate your accomplishments at the end of each lesson. Pay attention to teacher evaluations and comments.

	Unit Objectives (Lessons 1-5)	Lesson 1 (Date:_____)	Lesson 2 (Date:_____)
STEP 1	• Say the sounds for vowels ar, or, er, ir, ur. • Write the letters for the sounds / âr /, / ôr /, / êr /. • Identify syllables in words including <u>r</u>-controlled.	❏ Review: Vowels and Consonants ❏ Introduce: <u>r</u>-Controlled Syllables ❏ Vowel Chart ❏ Production/Replication ❏ Syllable Awareness: Segmentation	❏ Syllable Awareness: Segmentation ❏ Review: Conditions for Closed and <u>r</u>-Controlled Syllables ❏ Exercise 1: Listening for Sounds in Words
STEP 2	• Read fluently and spell words with sound spelling correspondences for this and previous units. • Read fluently and spell the **Essential Words**: day, little, may, new, say, way.	❏ Exercise 1: Spelling Pretest 1 ❏ Memorize It	❏ Exercise 2: Sort It: Closed and <u>r</u>-Controlled Syllables ❏ Word Fluency 1 ❏ Memorize It
STEP 3	• Identify synonyms, antonyms, and attributes for **Unit Words**. • Use comparative and superlative adjectives -er, -est.	❏ K-W-L Organizer ❏ Expression of the Day	❏ Introduce: Degrees of Adjectives ❏ Exercise 3: Rewrite It: Comparative Adjectives ❏ Expression of the Day
STEP 4	• Identify and use nouns, verbs, adjectives, and prepositions. • Identify complete subjects and complete predicates.	❏ Review: Singular and Plural Nouns ❏ Exercise 2: Identify It: Singular and Plural Nouns ❏ Review: Adjectives ❏ Exercise 3: Sort It: Adjectives	❏ Review: Noun, Verb, or Adjective ❏ Exercise 4: Identify It: Noun, Verb, or Adjective ❏ Review: Prepositions ❏ Exercise 5: Find It and Identify It: Prepositions
STEP 5	• Read phrases and passages fluently. • Preview reading selection using text features. • Define vocabulary using context-based strategies. • Read and understand informational text.	❏ Exercise 4: Phrase It ❏ Independent Text: **"Making Art"**	❏ Passage Fluency 1 ❏ Exercise 6: Use the Clues: Vocabulary Strategies
STEP 6	• Generate sentences using a six-stage process. • Distinguish fact and opinion statements. • Answer comprehension questions beginning with **infer, define, predict, generalize, use, explain, show** and **classify** in complete sentences based on text. • Organize ideas and information in a two-column outline for an expository (opinion) essay. • Write an expository (opinion) essay including an introduction and concluding paragraph.	❏ Masterpiece Sentences: Stages 1 and 2 ❏ Types of Statements: Fact or Opinion?	❏ Introduce: Attributes of an Opinion Essay Exercise 7: Analyze Opinion Essays
	Self-Evaluation (5 is the highest) **Effort** = I produced my best work. **Participation** = I was actively involved in tasks. **Independence** = I worked on my own.	**Effort:** 1 2 3 4 5 **Participation:** 1 2 3 4 5 **Independence:** 1 2 3 4 5	**Effort:** 1 2 3 4 5 **Participation:** 1 2 3 4 5 **Independence:** 1 2 3 4 5
	Teacher Evaluation	**Effort:** 1 2 3 4 5 **Participation:** 1 2 3 4 5 **Independence:** 1 2 3 4 5	**Effort:** 1 2 3 4 5 **Participation:** 1 2 3 4 5 **Independence:** 1 2 3 4 5

Lesson 3 (Date:_____)	**Lesson 4** (Date:_____)	**Lesson 5** (Date:_____)
❑ Syllable Awareness: Segmentation ❑ Exercise 1: Listening for Sounds in Words	❑ Exercise 1: Syllable Awareness: Segmentation	❑ Content Mastery: Syllable Awareness
❑ r-Controlled Syllables ❑ Exercise 2: Sort It: r-Controlled Syllables ❑ Review: Doubling Rule ❑ Double It ❑ Word Fluency 1	❑ Vowel Sounds and Spellings ❑ Exercise 2: Sort It: Sounds for o ❑ Divide It ❑ Word Fluency 2	❑ Content Mastery: Spelling Posttest 1
❑ Exercise 3: Define It ❑ Draw It: Idioms ❑ Expression of the Day	❑ Review: Degrees of Adjectives ❑ Exercise 3: Rewrite It: Superlative Adjectives ❑ Expression of the Day	❑ Review: Antonyms, Synonyms, and Attributes ❑ Introduce: Reading Word Pairs ❑ Exercise 1: Word Relationships: Antonyms, Synonyms, and Attributes ❑ Draw It: Idioms ❑ Expression of the Day
❑ Review: Prepositions and Prepositional Phrases ❑ Exercise 4: Identify It: Prepositional Phrases ❑ Review: The Verb Be ❑ Exercise 5: Rewrite It: Tense Forms of Be	❑ Review: Be as a Helping Verb ❑ Exercise 4: Choose It: Forms of Be ❑ Review: Using the Tense Timeline ❑ Exercise 5: Sort It: Past, Present, and Future Verbs	❑ Review: Complete Subject and Complete Predicate ❑ Exercise 2: Identify It: Complete Subject and Complete Predicate ❑ Masterpiece Sentences: Stage 4: Paint Your Subject ❑ Masterpiece Sentences: Using Adjectives
❑ Instructional Text: **"From Rock Art to Graffiti"** Exercise 6: Use the Clues: Vocabulary Strategies	❑ Writing an Introductory Paragraph for an Opinion Essay Exercise 6: Write It: Two-Sentence Introduction for Opinion Essay	❑ Prepare to Write: Expository (Opinion) Essay Exercise 3: Organize Information: Develop an Informal Outline
❑ Exercise 7: Answer It	❑ Prepare to Write: Expository (Opinion) Essay Exercise 7: Write It: Reasons to Support Your Opinion	❑ Organize Information: Develop an Informal Outline
Effort: 1 2 3 4 5 **Participation:** 1 2 3 4 5 **Independence:** 1 2 3 4 5	**Effort:** 1 2 3 4 5 **Participation:** 1 2 3 4 5 **Independence:** 1 2 3 4 5	**Effort:** 1 2 3 4 5 **Participation:** 1 2 3 4 5 **Independence:** 1 2 3 4 5
Effort: 1 2 3 4 5 **Participation:** 1 2 3 4 5 **Independence:** 1 2 3 4 5	**Effort:** 1 2 3 4 5 **Participation:** 1 2 3 4 5 **Independence:** 1 2 3 4 5	**Effort:** 1 2 3 4 5 **Participation:** 1 2 3 4 5 **Independence:** 1 2 3 4 5

Check off the activities you complete with each lesson. Evaluate your accomplishments at the end of each lesson. Pay attention to teacher evaluations and comments.

	Unit Objectives (Lessons 6-10)	Lesson 6 (Date:_____)	Lesson 7 (Date:_____)
STEP 1	• Say the sounds for vowels ar, or, er, ir, ur. • Write the letters for the sounds / âr /, / ôr /, / êr /. • Identify syllables in words including r-controlled. • Identify stressed syllables.	❑ Review: Stressed Syllables ❑ Exercise 1: Listening for Stressed Syllables	❑ Review: Shifting the Syllable Stress ❑ Exercise 1: Listening for Stressed Syllables
STEP 2	• Spell words with sound spelling correspondences for this and previous units. • Read fluently words with sound-spelling correspondences from this and previous units. • Read fluently the Essential Words: day, little, may, new, say, way. • Read and spell contractions with are.	❑ Exercise 2: Spelling Pretest 2 ❑ Word Fluency 3	❑ Multisyllable Words ❑ Exercise 2: Build It, Bank It ❑ Review: Contractions ❑ Exercise 3: Find It: Contractions
STEP 3	• Identify synonyms, antonyms, and attributes for Unit Words. • Use comparative and superlative adjectives -er, -est.	❑ Review: Antonyms, Synonyms, and Attributes ❑ Exercise 3: Word Relationships: Antonyms, Synonyms, and Attributes ❑ Expression of the Day	❑ Review: Prefixes ❑ Introduce: Prefixes inter- and under- ❑ Exercise 4: Match It: Prefixes ❑ Expression of the Day
STEP 4	• Identify and use nouns, verbs, adjectives, and prepositions. • Identify complete subjects and complete predicates. • Form sentences with compound parts using or.	❑ Review: Complete Subject and Complete Predicate ❑ Review: Compound Subjects and Compound Predicates ❑ Exercise 4: Combine It: Compound Subjects ❑ Exercise 5: Combine It: Compound Predicates	❑ Review: Diagram It: Subject + Verb ❑ Review: Compound Subjects ❑ Exercise 5: Diagram It: Compound Subjects
STEP 5	• Read phrases and passages fluently. • Preview reading selection using text features. • Define vocabulary using context-based strategies. • Read and understand informational text.	❑ Exercise 6: Phrase It ❑ Independent Text: "Art at Home and Art in Caves" Exercise 7: Use the Clues: Vocabulary Strategies	❑ Passage Fluency 2 ❑ Exercise 6: Use the Clues: Vocabulary Strategies
STEP 6	• Answer comprehension questions beginning with infer, define, predict, generalize, use, explain, show and classify in complete sentences based on text. • Write an expository (opinion) essay including an introduction and concluding paragraph. • Edit and revise an expository (opinion) essay.	❑ Exercise 8: Rewrite It: Using Synonyms	❑ Report Structure
	Self-Evaluation (5 is the highest) **Effort** = I produced my best work. **Participation** = I was actively involved in tasks. **Independence** = I worked on my own.	**Effort:** 1 2 3 4 5 **Participation:** 1 2 3 4 5 **Independence:** 1 2 3 4 5	**Effort:** 1 2 3 4 5 **Participation:** 1 2 3 4 5 **Independence:** 1 2 3 4 5
	Teacher Evaluation	**Effort:** 1 2 3 4 5 **Participation:** 1 2 3 4 5 **Independence:** 1 2 3 4 5	**Effort:** 1 2 3 4 5 **Participation:** 1 2 3 4 5 **Independence:** 1 2 3 4 5

Lesson 8 (Date:_____)	Lesson 9 (Date:_____)	Lesson 10 (Date:_____)
❑ Exercise 1: Listening for Word Parts	❑ Exercise 1: Listening for Stressed Syllables	❑ Exercise 1: Syllable Awareness: Segmentation
❑ Divide It ❑ Exercise 2: Sort It: Final Sounds ❑ Word Fluency 4	❑ Review: Prefixes ❑ Exercise 2: Build It	❑ Content Mastery: Spelling Posttest 2
❑ Content Mastery: Word Relationships and Morphology	❑ Review: Prefixes ❑ Exercise 3: Find It: Prefixes ❑ Exercises 3 and 4: Use the Clues: Vocabulary Strategies ❑ Expression of the Day	❑ Exercise 2: Match It: Homophones ❑ Draw It: Idioms ❑ Expression of the Day ❑ K-W-L Organizer
❑ Review: Diagram It: Subject + Verb ❑ Review: Compound Predicate ❑ Exercise 3: Diagram It: Compound Predicate	❑ Review: Compound Subjects and Compound Predicates ❑ Exercise 5: Revise It: Compound Subjects and Compound Predicates	❑ Content Mastery: Parts of Speech; Complete Subjects and Predicates; Compound Subjects and Predicates
❑ Instructional Text: "Becoming an Artist" Exercise 4: Use the Clues: Vocabulary Strategies	❑ Write It: Expository (Opinion) Essay	❑ Write a Concluding Paragraph for an Expository (Opinion) Essay
❑ Exercise 5: Answer It: Using Signal Words	❑ Write It: Expository (Opinion) Essay	❑ Check It: Draft of an Expository (Opinion) Report
Effort: 1 2 3 4 5 **Participation:** 1 2 3 4 5 **Independence:** 1 2 3 4 5	**Effort:** 1 2 3 4 5 **Participation:** 1 2 3 4 5 **Independence:** 1 2 3 4 5	**Effort:** 1 2 3 4 5 **Participation:** 1 2 3 4 5 **Independence:** 1 2 3 4 5
Effort: 1 2 3 4 5 **Participation:** 1 2 3 4 5 **Independence:** 1 2 3 4 5	**Effort:** 1 2 3 4 5 **Participation:** 1 2 3 4 5 **Independence:** 1 2 3 4 5	**Effort:** 1 2 3 4 5 **Participation:** 1 2 3 4 5 **Independence:** 1 2 3 4 5

Exercise 1 · Spelling Pretest 1

▸ Write the words your teacher says.

1. _____	6. _____	11. _____
2. _____	7. _____	12. _____
3. _____	8. _____	13. _____
4. _____	9. _____	14. _____
5. _____	10. _____	15. _____

Exercise 2 · Identify It: Singular and Plural Nouns

▸ Read each sentence.

▸ Decide if the underlined word is singular or plural.

▸ Put an X in the column to mark your answer.

	Singular	Plural
1. Michael loves making <u>quilts</u>.		
2. If you have a <u>pen</u>, you might sketch.		
3. Lines become <u>shapes</u>.		
4. Your work turns into <u>art</u>!		
5. Where are your <u>notes</u>?		

Exercise 3 · Sort It: Adjectives

▶ Read each sentence. An adjective in it is underlined.

▶ Decide which question the adjective answers.

▶ Write the adjective in the correct column.

1. Cummings created <u>colorful</u> quilts.

2. He became a <u>big</u> fan of fabric.

3. He made <u>vivid</u> images of butterflies.

4. <u>One</u> sculpture is called *The Harp*.

5. Calder made <u>many</u> mobiles.

6. Elisa made <u>those</u> artworks from common scraps.

7. She turned caps from drinks into <u>small</u> pans.

8. Elisa collected bits of <u>colored</u> rags.

9. These make a <u>dozen</u> shapes in her new book.

10. Twine made a <u>first-rate</u> bird's nest.

Which One?	What Kind?	How Many?

Unit 14 · Lesson 1

Exercise 4 · Phrase It

▸ Read each sentence.

▸ Use a pencil to "scoop" the phrases in each sentence.

▸ Read each sentences as you would speak it.

▸ The first two are done for you.

1. Sketching is a basic form of art.

2. You're expressing yourself by making art.

3. The bell rings and class begins.

4. Others begin to take notes.

5. You begin to sketch.

6. Your lines become art.

7. Notes will help you pass the test.

8. It's hard to sketch and take notes.

9. Keron began sketching figures.

10. Keron's sketches led him to success.

Exercise 1 · Listening for Sounds in Words

▶ Listen to the word your teacher says.

▶ Identify the **r**-controlled vowel sound.

▶ Mark the **vowel** before the **r** with a circumflex (^).

1. ar   er   or

2. ar   er   or

3. ar   er   or

4. ar   er   or

5. ar   er   or

6. ar   er   or

7. ar   er   or

8. ar   er   or

9. ar   er   or

10. ar   er   or

11. ar   er   or

12. ar   er   or

13. ar   er   or

14. ar   er   or

15. ar   er   or

Unit 14 · Lesson 2

Exercise 2 · Sort It: Closed and r-Controlled Syllables

▸ Read each word in the **Word Bank**.

▸ Sort each word according to its syllable type.

▸ Write the words under the correct heading.

Word Bank

pat	hut	part	port	bird
bid	chart	north	for	hurt
art	her	mark	chat	pot
girl	star	turn	short	form

Closed Syllable	r-Controlled Syllables		
short vowels	/ âr /	/ ôr /	/ êr /

Exercise 3 · Rewrite It: Comparative Adjectives

▸ Read each adjective.

▸ Add **-er** to make the comparative form of each adjective.

    1. sick _____

    2. dark _____

    3. short _____

    4. fast _____

    5. smart _____

▸ Read the comparative adjectives from above.

▸ Choose and write the appropriate comparative adjective from above to complete each item below.

    1. Complete this sentence.

    The kitchen is _____ than the living room, because it has only one window.

    2. Finish the antonym pair.

    taller : _____

    3. Finish the synonym pair.

    quicker : _____

    4. Write a sentence using a comparative adjective.

    _____

    5. Write a word that rhymes.

    quicker : _____

Unit 14 · Lesson 2

Exercise 4 · Identify It: Noun, Verb, or Adjective

▶ Read each sentence.

▶ Look at the underlined word in each sentence.

▶ Use the context to decide if the underlined word is a noun, verb, or adjective.

▶ Fill in the correct bubble.

▶ Read these examples with your teacher.

	noun	verb	adjective
Examples: The women opened her <u>compact</u>.	◯	◯	◯
We <u>compact</u> our trash.	◯	◯	◯
We took a <u>compact</u> stove to the park.	◯	◯	◯

	noun	verb	adjective
1. I sent a <u>short</u> note to my pal.	◯	◯	◯
2. The <u>short</u> in the TV shot sparks out.	◯	◯	◯
3. They <u>short</u> us on our pay, and we gripe.	◯	◯	◯
4. The helpers <u>light</u> the candles.	◯	◯	◯
5. We had a <u>light</u> snack.	◯	◯	◯
6. The <u>light</u> here is harsh.	◯	◯	◯
7. She hit a shot with one <u>second</u> left.	◯	◯	◯
8. This is my <u>second</u> glass of milk.	◯	◯	◯

(continued)

Exercise 4 (continued) · Identify It: Noun, Verb, or Adjective

	noun	verb	adjective
9. I <u>second</u> the nomination.	◯	◯	◯
10. Abdul is a <u>top</u> student.	◯	◯	◯

Exercise 5 · Find It and Identify It: Prepositions

▸ Read the short passages.

▸ Highlight each preposition.

▸ Determine whether the preposition shows position in space, position in time, or neither.

▸ Record the preposition in the correct column.

> **based on "Becoming an Artist" and "From Rock Art to Graffiti"**
>
> At 17, Augusta Savage knew she wanted to be an artist. In 1921, she moved to New York and lived in Harlem. As an artist, she won many awards.
>
> Keith Haring was from New York. Haring began drawing graffiti on the streets. He invented his own tag, or signature. He left his tag near each drawing.

Position in Space	Position in Time	Neither

Exercise 6 · Use the Clues: Vocabulary Strategies

▸ Read each sentence pair.

▸ Identify the pronoun in the second sentence and circle it.

▸ Identify the noun the pronoun is replacing in each sentence and underline it.

▸ Draw an arrow to link the pronoun to the noun it replaced.

1. Meet Michael A. Cummings. He was born in Los Angeles.

2. Cummings bought a sewing machine. Cummings used it for making quilts.

3. Augusta Savage had students. Savage inspired them to make art.

4. Calder invented the mobile. The mobile was his form of art.

5. Picasso said children were artists. Picasso said they could see the world with new eyes.

Exercise 7 · Analyze Opinion Essays

▸ Read the pro opinion essay.

▸ Read the **introductory paragraph**. Underline the words that show the writer's opinion. Number the reasons that support the position of the writer.

▸ Identify the **transition topic sentences** in the body paragraphs and highlight them in yellow. Number them to show the connection to the reasons in the introductory paragraph. Circle the transitions.

▸ Read the **concluding paragraph**. Underline the words that restate the writer's opinion.

▸ Repeat these steps with the con opinion essay.

Opinion Essay (Pro)

I think the school should let art students paint a mural in the cafeteria. A mural will make the cafeteria more colorful and will give art students a chance to share their talents with the school. 〉 **Introductory Paragraph**

One reason I am in favor of the mural is that it will make the cafeteria walls more colorful and interesting. The plain blue paint on the walls is boring to look at. A mural will bring color into the room. It will give students something interesting to look at and talk about as they eat.

In addition, letting art students paint a mural will give them a chance to share their talents with the school. Students don't usually get to use their artistic talents outside of art class. Painting a mural will let students share their ideas and creativity. Whenever anyone looks at the mural, they will remember the students who painted it and be glad those students made the school more interesting. 〉 **Body Paragraphs**

Letting art students paint a mural is a great idea. A colorful mural in the cafeteria would be a great gift to the school and would allow students to share their talents. 〉 **Concluding Paragraph**

(continued)

Exercise 7 (continued) · Analyze Opinion Essays

Opinion Essay (Con)

> I do not think it is a good idea to let students paint a mural in the cafeteria. They could paint weird things in the mural and make a mess.　　**Introductory Paragraph**

> First, the art students could paint weird things in the mural that would make the cafeteria ugly. Some people like strange pictures that others don't. My little brother loves to draw pictures of spiders, explosions, and other horrible things. Students like my brother might paint something gross like a giant snake because they think it is cool. This would make the cafeteria ugly and unpleasant.
>
> Second, painting a mural would make a big mess. Paint would get everywhere. The school would need to close part of the cafeteria to keep students away from the mural. There might not be enough room for everyone to sit and eat lunch. It would take a long time to finish the mural. The cafeteria could be a disaster all year.　　**Body Paragraphs**

> Letting the art students paint a mural could cause a lot of problems. We should leave the cafeteria walls the way they are now.　　**Concluding Paragraph**

▶ What are two attributes of an opinion essay?

1. _____

2. _____

Exercise 1 · Listening for Sounds in Words

▸ Listen to each word your teacher says.

▸ Write the letter or letters where you hear the designated sound.

1.

2.

3.

4.

5.

6.

7.

8.

9.

10.

Unit 14 · Lesson 3

Exercise 2 · Sort It: <u>r</u>-Controlled Syllables

▸ Read the words in the **Word Bank**.

▸ Sort the words with <u>r</u>-controlled syllables according to their vowel sound and spelling.

▸ Write each word under the correct heading.

Word Bank

burn	short	bar	dark	verb
her	bird	fern	first	star
girl	stir	church	corn	hurt

/ êr / = ir	/ êr / = er	/ êr / = ur	/ âr / = ar	/ ôr / = or

Exercise 3 · Define It

▶ Fill in the blanks with a category and an attribute to define each word.

▶ If you are unsure of your definition, compare it with the word's definition in a dictionary.

▶ Do the first definition with your teacher.

1. An **artist** is _____ who _____
   category   attribute(s)

   _____

   _____ .

2. A **car** is _____ that _____
   category   attribute(s)

   _____

   _____ .

3. A **porch** is _____ that _____
   category   attribute(s)

   _____

   _____ .

4. **Corn** is _____ that _____
   category   attribute(s)

   _____

   _____ .

5. A **desert** is _____ that _____
   category   attribute(s)

   _____

   _____ .

6. A **farm** is _____ that _____
   category   attribute(s)

   _____

   _____ .

(continued)

Exercise 3 (continued) · **Define It**

7. A **garden** is _____ that _____
    category   attribute(s)

    _____

    _____.

8. A **horse** is _____ that _____
    category   attribute(s)

    _____

    _____.

9. A **park** is _____ that _____
    category   attribute(s)

    _____

    _____.

10. A **river** is _____ that _____
    category   attribute(s)

    _____

    _____.

▸ Which vocabulary words are related to land? Write the words in the blanks.

_____   _____   _____

_____

Exercise 4 · Identify It: Prepositional Phrases

▸ Read each sentence.

▸ Reread the prepositional phrase that is underlined in each sentence.

▸ Circle the preposition.

▸ Put an X in the correct column to show what the prepositional phrase shows.

	Position in Space	Position in Time
1. Just sit and think <u>in the yard</u>.		
2. You must come <u>before</u> noon.		
3. Take notes <u>during first period</u>.		
4. Sketch <u>after dinner</u>.		
5. It's hard to sketch and take notes <u>at the same time</u>.		
6. Your sketch paper is <u>inside the cabinet</u>.		
7. The brushes are <u>on the sink</u>.		
8. You may paint <u>until 10 o'clock</u>.		
9. <u>Since last Sunday</u>, Jim has been painting every day.		
10. His best painting hangs <u>beside the door</u>.		

Exercise 5 · Rewrite It: Tense Forms of *Be*

▶ Read the sentence in the first column. Circle the subject and underline the form of **be** used with it.

▶ Change the verb to the new tense listed in the middle column. Use the form of **be** that goes with the subject of the sentence.

▶ Look at the charts in the Handbook section of the *Student Text* to be sure you have chosen the correct form of **be**.

Sentence	New Tense	New Sentence
Example: You are a fine partner.	Past Tense	You _____ a fine partner.
Example: I was an expert.	Present Tense	I _____ an expert.
1. She is a doctor.	Past Tense	She _____ a doctor.
2. We were observers.	Present Tense	We _____ observers.
3. You were so charming!	Present Tense	You _____ so charming!
4. I am an explorer.	Past Tense	I _____ an explorer.
5. He was a summer intern.	Present Tense	He _____ a summer intern.
6. They are forgetful.	Past Tense	They _____ forgetful.
7. We are art critics.	Past Tense	We _____ art critics.
8. I was a club member.	Present Tense	I _____ a club member.
9. They were clerks in the shop.	Present Tense	They _____ clerks in the shop.
10. You are a helpful partner.	Past Tense	You _____ a helpful partner.

Exercise 6 · Use the Clues: Vocabulary Strategies

▶ Use meaning signals to define **pictographs** and **engravings**.

- Underline the vocabulary words.

- Read the text before and after the unknown words.

- Double underline the word or words that help define each unknown word.

- Circle the meaning signal words.

---

based on "From Rock Art to Graffiti"

Early types of rock art are *pictographs*. These are drawings or paintings on rocks. The painter uses fingers or a brush. *Engravings* are forms of rock art. The rock surface is cut. This leaves pictures on the rock.

▶ Write a definition based on the context clues.

pictographs— _____

_____

engravings— _____

_____

▶ Verify your definition with the dictionary or an online reference.

▶ Draw arrows from the underlined vocabulary words to the underlined definitions.

Exercise 7 · Answer It

▸ Underline the signal word in the question.

▸ Write the answer in complete sentences.

▸ Check for sentence signals—capital letters, commas, and end punctuation.

1. There are many types of rock art. What can you infer about the types of tools used to create engravings, petroglyphs, and sculptures?

   _____

   _____

   _____

   _____

2. Define **muralist** in your own words.

   _____

   _____

   _____

3. Using a timeline, show the progression of rock art from prehistoric cave paintings to modern graffiti.

Past		Present

(continued)

4. The text describes how rock art has changed throughout history. Predict what art form will be most popular in 10 years.

_____

_____

_____

5. A metaphor is a figure of speech that compares people, places, things, or feelings without using the words **like** or **as**. The phrase "the electricity of his work" is a metaphor. Explain what this metaphor tells you about Haring's art.

_____

_____

_____

Exercise 1 · Syllable Awareness: Segmentation

▸ Listen to the word your teacher says.

▸ Count the syllables. Write the number of syllables in the first column.

▸ Write the letter or letters for each vowel sound you hear.

▸ Mark short vowels with a breve (˘).

▸ For **r**-controlled vowels, mark the vowel before the **r** with a circumflex (^).

How many syllables do you hear?	First vowel sound	Second vowel sound	Third vowel sound
1.			
2.			
3.			
4.			
5.			
6.			
7.			
8.			
9.			
10.			

Exercise 2 · Sort It: Sounds for <u>o</u>

▶ Read each word in the **Word Bank**.

▶ Sort each word according to the sound represented by the letter **o**.

▶ Write the word in the chart under the correct heading.

Word Bank

born	correct	mother	brother
morning	cover	north	monster
other	shorter	another	modern
optical	wonder	boxcar	core

o = / ŭ / + er	o + r = / ôr /	o = / ŏ /

Unit 14 · Lesson 4

▸ Read each adjective.

▸ Add **-est** to make its superlative form.

1. sick _____

2. dark _____

3. short _____

4. fast _____

5. smart _____

▸ Choose and write an appropriate superlative adjective from above to complete each item below.

1. Complete the sentence.

   She was the _____ of those who had the flu.

2. Finish the antonym pair.

   tallest: _____

3. Finish the synonym pair.

   quickest: _____

4. Write a sentence using a superlative adjective from the list above.

   _____

5. Write the comparative form of the last adjective in the list.

   _____

Exercise 4 · Choose It: Forms of Be

▸ Read and complete the first sentence with your teacher.

▸ Read each sentence with your teacher.

▸ Choose the correct form of **be** in parentheses to complete the sentence. Use the charts below to help you.

▸ Write the correct form in the blank.

Correct Use of Present Tense Forms of Be		
Pronouns	*Singular*	*Plural*
First Person	I **am** snacking.	We **are** snacking.
Second Person	You **are** snacking.	You **are** snacking.
Third Person	He (She, It) **is** snacking.	They **are** snacking.

Correct Use of Past Tense Forms of Be		
Pronouns	*Singular*	*Plural*
First Person	I **was** snacking.	We **were** snacking.
Second Person	You **were** snacking.	You **were** snacking.
Third Person	He (She, It) **was** snacking.	They **were** snacking.

1. Yesterday morning my sisters_____ cutting up apples. (was, were)

2. Yolanda _____ directing Maria and Berta. (was, be)

3. Yolanda_____taking a cooking class at school. (is, am)

4. The girls _____fixing a big salad for lunch. (been, were)

5. At 1:00 PM yesterday, Maria and Berta_____ bringing plates of salad to everyone in the family. (was, were)

6. Now Yolanda_____starting another project. (is, be)

7. She and my other sisters_____ collecting twigs and branches. (am, are)

8. You_____wondering what dish they can make from those things, aren't you? (be, are)

9. The three girls_____making a display for a birthday party. (is, are)

10. I_____looking forward to that gathering. (am, are)

Unit 14 · Lesson 4

Exercise 5 · Sort It: Past, Present, and Future Verbs

▸ Read each verb and verb phrase in the **Word Bank**.

▸ Identify the time conveyed by this word or phrase.

▸ Record the verb or verb phrase under the correct position on the **Tense Timeline**.

▸ The first one is done for you.

Word Bank

was marking	is coloring	burns
harvested	infers	am hammering
occurred	will permit	were serving
will understand	marketed	will be entering
will chart	are hurting	will be interacting

Yesterday	Today	Tomorrow
Past	**Present**	**Future**
1.	1.	1.
2.	2.	2.
3.	3.	3.
4.	4.	4.
5.	5.	5.

Exercise 6 · Write It: Two-Sentence Introduction for Opinion Essays

▸ Read each prompt and position below.

▸ Mark the prompt by underlining the signal words and double underlining the topic.

▸ Read the star ideas with suggested reasons.

▸ Write a sentence that states the topic and the writer's opinion. The first one has been done as an example.

▸ Write a sentence that states the plan based on the star ideas. Use **and** to connect your ideas. The first one has been done as an example.

▸ Then write the two sentences together to finish the two-sentence introduction.

1. **Prompt:** Write an essay giving your opinion and stating reasons whether or not the school should let students paint a mural in the cafeteria.

   Position: (pro) the school should let art students paint a mural in the cafeteria

   Star ideas: ★ cafeteria more colorful
      ★ a way for student artists to share their talent

   State the Topic: I think the school should let art students paint a mural in the cafeteria.

   State the Plan: A mural will make the cafeteria more colorful and gives art students a chance to share their talents with the school.

   Two-Sentence Introduction: _____

   _____

   _____

   _____

   _____

2. **Prompt:** Write an essay to explain whether or not you think students should get a discounted rate for admission to museums.

   Position: (pro) students should get a discounted rate for admission to museums

   Star ideas: ★ encourages learning
      ★ makes it possible for students with limited money to attend

(continued)

Exercise 6 (continued) · Write It: Two-Sentence Introduction for Opinion Essays

State the Topic: _____

_____

State the Plan: _____

_____

_____

Two-Sentence Introduction: _____

_____

_____

_____

_____

3. **Prompt:** State your opinion about sports figures endorsing products. Do you think sports figures should endorse products or not?

Position: (con) disagree that sports figures should endorse products

Star ideas: ★ encourages potentially unnecessary spending
★ endorsements suggest a better product, which may not be true

State the Topic: _____

_____

State the Plan: _____

_____

_____

Two-Sentence Introduction: _____

_____

_____

_____

_____

Unit 14 · Lesson 4

Exercise 7 · Write It: Reasons to Support Your Opinion

▶ Read and mark each prompt by underlining the signal word and double underlining the topic.

▶ Write the topic and position in the space provided.

▶ Brainstorm possible reasons to support your position. Write them next to the stars.

1. **Prompt:** Write an essay describing your opinion about content ratings for music CD's. Do you think ratings provide valuable information or not?

   Topic and Position: _____

   _____

   ★ _____

   ★ _____

2. **Prompt:** Write an essay explaining your opinion on curfews. Are they a good way to keep teens safe and out of trouble, or are they an insult to responsible teens?

   Topic and Position: _____

   _____

   ★ _____

   ★ _____

3. **Prompt:** Imagine your town government is considering selling your neighborhood playing field for an office complex development. Write an essay explaining your position about this plan. Are you for or against the sale of the field?

   Topic and Position: _____

   _____

   ★ _____

   ★ _____

Exercise 1 • Word Relationships: Antonyms, Synonyms, and Attributes

Antonyms

▸ Read the words in the **Word Bank**.

▸ For each numbered word, choose and write the word from the **Word Bank** that is an antonym (opposite).

▸ Read the word pairs. Discuss your answers.

Word Bank

summer	send	over
after	long	import

1. short : _____

2. under : _____

3. winter : _____

4. export : _____

5. before : _____

Synonyms

▸ Read the words in the **Word Bank**.

▸ For each numbered word, choose and write the word from the **Word Bank** that is a synonym (same or almost the same).

▸ Read the word pairs. Discuss your answers.

Word Bank

spin	after	method
occur	send	rug

(continued)

Exercise 1 (continued) · Word Networks: Antonyms, Synonyms, and Attributes

6. carpet : _____

7. twirl : _____

8. export : _____

9. happen : _____

10. way : _____

Attributes

▶ Read the words in the **Word Bank**.

▶ For each numbered word, choose and write the word from the **Word Bank** that is an attribute (shows a relationship or association).

▶ Read the word pairs. Discuss your answers.

Word Bank

morning	current	long
plant	pancake	bumper

11. river : _____

12. corn : _____

13. car : _____

14. breakfast : _____

15. day : _____

Unit 14 · Lesson 5

Exercise 2 · Identify It: Complete Subject and Complete Predicate

▸ Read each sentence.

▸ Identify the complete subject. Underline it once.

▸ Identify the complete predicate. Underline it twice.

1. Early humans created rock art.

2. Rock art has changed over time.

3. Mexican artists created murals.

4. These murals were painted on walls.

5. Graffiti artists create a form of rock art.

6. One famous artist drew with chalk.

7. Pyramids and flying saucers appeared on black panels.

8. The black panels covered old ads.

9. Subway riders saw the chalk drawings.

10. The artist became famous for his lively drawings.

Exercise 3 · Organize Information: Develop an Informal Outline

▶ Read the following prompt. Underline the signal words once and the topic twice

In order to cut the budget, the school district is thinking about eliminating art classes. Write a multiparagraph essay stating your position about eliminating art classes. Give reasons to support your position.

▶ Think about how you would feel if your principal proposed eliminating art. Would you be for it (pro) or against it (con)? Write your answer on the following line.

_____

▶ Fill out the informal outline. Begin by choosing star ideas (reasons) for the left side of the outline, and then choose E's (examples, elaboration, and evidence) for the right side.

Topic: _____

★ _____   — _____

    _____   • _____

                                   • _____

                                   — _____

                                   • _____

                                   • _____

★ _____   — _____

    _____   • _____

                                   • _____

                                   — _____

                                   • _____

                                   • _____

▶ Use the outline to draft a **Two-Sentence Introductory Paragraph**.

_____

_____

_____

Exercise 1 · Listening for Stressed Syllables

▸ Listen to the word your teacher says.

▸ Repeat the word.

▸ Listen for the stressed syllable.

▸ Mark an X in the box to mark the position of the stressed syllable.

	1st Syllable	2nd Syllable
Example: sculpture		
1. explore		
2. under		
3. summer		
4. wonder		
5. harvest		

Exercise 2 · Spelling Pretest 2

▸ Write the words your teacher says.

1. _____   6. _____   11. _____

2. _____   7. _____   12. _____

3. _____   8. _____   13. _____

4. _____   9. _____   14. _____

5. _____   10. _____   15. _____

Exercise 3 · Word Relationships: Antonyms, Synonyms, and Attributes

▶ Read each word pair.

▶ Write the word pair in the column that describes the relationship.

▶ Discuss your answers with a partner.

import : export	export : send	over : under	corn : harvest
river : current	before : after	happen : occur	flower : plant
way : method	day : morning	short : long	winter : summer

Antonyms (opposite)	Synonyms (same)	Attributes (associations)

Exercise 4 · Combine It: Compound Subjects

▸ Read each pair of sentences.

▸ Combine the sentences using the conjunction in parentheses.

▸ Write the new sentence.

▸ Circle both simple subjects in the sentence you write.

1. The doctor will help them. The nurse will help them. (and)

_____

2. Calder made art. Picasso made art. (and)

_____

3. Shops have murals. Hotels have murals. (and)

_____

4. Yarn can make fantastic art. Twine can make fantastic art. (or)

_____

5. Graffiti make an interesting exhibit. Wall paintings make an interesting exhibit. (or)

_____

Exercise 5 · Combine It: Compound Predicates

▸ Read each pair of sentences.

▸ Combine these sentences using the conjunction in parentheses.

▸ Write the new sentence.

▸ Circle both verbs in the sentence you write.

1. An artist sculpts stone. An artist carves stone. (or)

_____

2. Calder imagined the mobile. Calder invented the mobile. (and)

_____

3. The cave dwellers hunted. The cave dwellers fished. (and)

_____

4. People etched on cave walls. People drew on cave walls. (or)

_____

5. Water did not hurt the etchings. Water did not wash away the etchings. (or)

_____

Exercise 6 · Phrase It

▸ Use a pencil to "scoop" the phrases in each sentence.

▸ Then read each sentence as you would say it.

▸ The first two sentences are done for you.

1. Elisa used scraps to make art.

2. Elisa's scraps became 3-D art.

3. Elisa had discovered something.

4. Common scraps can make fantastic art.

5. The first form of art was cave art.

6. A hundred tales are told in cave art.

7. Cave art tells the tales of cave people.

8. The cave dwellers hunted and fished.

9. They made messages for each other.

10. From cave art, we learn history.

Exercise 7 · Use the Clues: Vocabulary Strategies

▸ Read the excerpt based on **"Art at Home and Art in Caves."**

▸ Read the underlined phrase in the paragraph.

▸ Circle the word or words in the paragraph that are substituted for the underlined phrase.

▸ Record substitutions on the lines below the text.

---

based on "Art at Home and Art in Caves"

Where Did Art Start?

The first form of art was cave art. <u>**Cave artists**</u> made lots of sketches inside caves. Cave art tells the tales of the lives of cave people. The cave dwellers hunted and fished. They made messages for each other. The art they made is still there. The messages they left us tell us much. From cave art, we learn history. We learn about the lives of some of the first humans. We learn something even more important. We learn that humans have always been engaged with making art.

Substitutions for **cave artists**: _____

_____

Unit 14 · Lesson 6

▸ Read the following sentences.

▸ Substitute the underlined word(s) with a synonym or phrase that means the same thing.

▸ Rewrite the sentences.

▸ Check for sentence signals—capital letters and end punctuation.

▸ Read the new sentences.

1. <u>Fame</u> was in store for Elisa Kleven.

_____

2. She began to tell <u>little tales</u>.

_____

3. Common scraps can make <u>fantastic</u> art.

_____

4. Cave artists made a lot of <u>sketches</u> inside caves.

_____

5. They <u>made messages for</u> each other.

_____

Exercise 1 · Listening for Stressed Syllables

▶ Listen to the word your teacher says. Repeat the word.

▶ Listen for the stressed, or accented, syllable.

▶ Put an X in the box to mark the position of the stressed syllable.

1. ☐☐   6. ☐☐

2. ☐☐   7. ☐☐

3. ☐☐   8. ☐☐

4. ☐☐   9. ☐☐

5. ☐☐   10. ☐☐

Exercise 2 · Build It, Bank It

▸ Read the syllables in the box.

▸ Circle the prefixes.

▸ Combine each prefix with a base word or root to make a word. Try to make as many words as possible.

▸ Record the words on the lines below.

▸ Check a dictionary to verify that the words you wrote are real words.

pass	inter	stand	ject
shirt	mit	pret	under
act	brush	hand	est

_____   _____

_____   _____

_____   _____

_____   _____

_____   _____

Exercise 3 · Find It: Contractions

▸ Read the sentences.

▸ Circle the contractions.

▸ Expand each contraction into two words.

1. We're interested in ordering another pattern. _____

2. Perhaps they're covering their artwork with the plastic. _____

3. You're permitted to enter over there. _____

4. We're trying to understand your book order. _____

5. They're interacting very well with the third doctor. _____

Unit 14 · Lesson 7

Exercise 4 · Match It: Prefixes

▸ Use what you know about the prefix **inter-** to figure out the meaning of each numbered word.

▸ Draw a line to match the word to the correct definition.

▸ Use a dictionary to verify the definitions.

Words	Definitions
1. Internet	**a.** to break into a conversation among people
2. interconnected	**b.** between or among nations
3. interstellar	**c.** between or among the stars
4. interrupt	**d.** having links between or among people or things
5. international	**e.** a network between and among people

▸ Look at the definitions for items 1–5. What words do the definitions have in common?

Inter- means: _____.

▸ Use what you know about the prefix **under-** to figure out the meaning of each numbered word.

▸ Draw a line to match the word to the correct definition.

▸ Use a dictionary to verify the definitions.

Words	Definitions
6. underbid	**f.** to charge below the price; to not charge enough
7. undercharge	**g.** to shoot below or shorter than the needed distance
8. underhand	**h.** beneath or below
9. undershoot	**i.** to offer an amount below others or below cost
10. under	**j.** to throw by swinging the hand below the shoulder

▸ Look at definitions for items 6–10. What words do they have in common?

Under- means: _____.

Exercise 5 · Diagram It: Compound Subjects

▶ Review these areas of the diagram with your teacher:

1. **Subject:**   Who (what) did it?

2. **Verb:**   What did they (he, she, it) do?

3. **Direct Object:**   Who (what) did they (he, she, it) do it to?

▶ Read each sentence. The simple subjects in the compound subject are underlined.

▶ Write each word in the correct place on the diagram.

1. The <u>doctor</u> or the <u>nurse</u> will help.

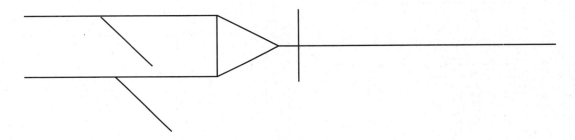

2. <u>Calder</u> and <u>Picasso</u> made art.

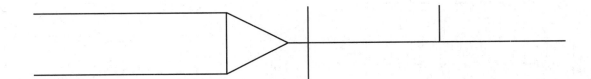

(continued)

Exercise 5 *(continued)* · Diagram It: Compound Subjects

3. <u>Shops</u> and <u>hotels</u> have murals.

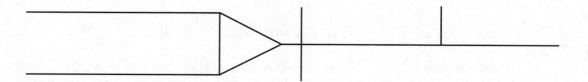

4. <u>Yarn</u> or <u>twine</u> can make fantastic art.

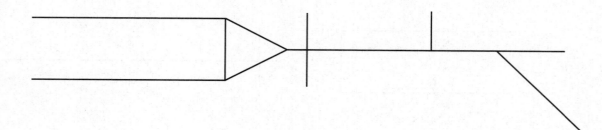

5. <u>Graffiti</u> or wall <u>paintings</u> make an interesting exhibit.

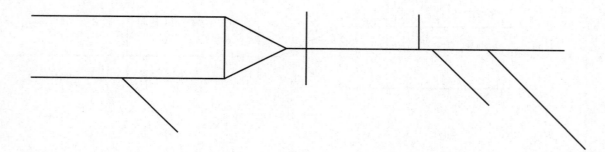

Exercise 6 · Use the Clues: Vocabulary Strategies

▸ Read the passage.

▸ Reread the underlined sentences.

▸ Draw an arrow from the circled pronouns to the words they represent.

based on "Art at Home and Art in Caves"

Fame was in store for Elisa Kleven. (She)₁ made a name for herself. It began when she was a little girl. Common scraps fascinated (her.)₂ (She)₃ used scraps to make art. Nutshells became beds. Caps from drinks became small baking pans. (She)₄ loved to make little settings. The settings Elisa created inspired her. (She)₅ began to tell little tales.

Exercise 1 · Listening for Word Parts

▸ Listen to each word your teacher says.

▸ Mark whether or not you hear a suffix.

▸ If yes, spell the suffix.

	Do you hear a suffix on the word?		If yes, spell the suffix.
	Yes	**No**	
1.			
2.			
3.			
4.			
5.			
6.			
7.			
8.			
9.			
10.			

Exercise 2 · Sort It: Final Sounds

▸ Read the words in the **Word Bank**.

▸ Work with a partner.

▸ Sort the words according to their final sounds.

▸ Label the headings.

Word Bank

carve	horse	serve	starve
verse	observe	forgive	remorse
have	nurse	give	purse

Unit 14 · Lesson 8

Exercise 3 · Diagram It: Compound Predicate

▸ Review these areas of the diagram with your teacher:

1. Subject: Who (what) did it?

2. Verb: What did they (he, she, it) do?

3. Direct Object: Who (what) did they (he, she, it) do it to?

▸ Read each sentence. The two verbs in the compound predicate are underlined.

▸ Write each word in the correct place on the diagram.

1. An artist <u>carves</u> or <u>sculpts</u> stone.

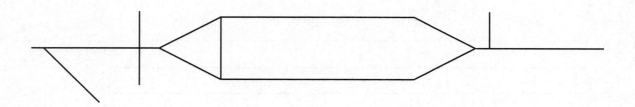

2. Calder <u>imagined</u> and <u>invented</u> the mobile.

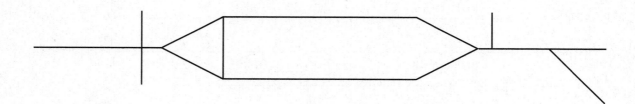

(continued)

Exercise 3 *(continued)* · **Diagram It: Compound Predicate**

3. The cave dwellers <u>hunted</u> and <u>fished</u>.

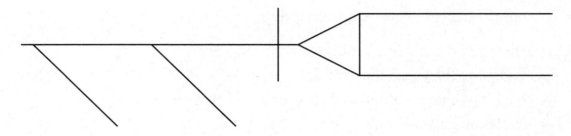

4. People <u>etched</u> or <u>drew</u> marks on cave walls.

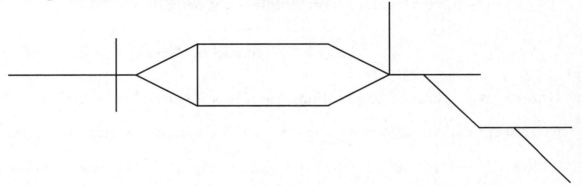

5. Water <u>did</u> not <u>hurt</u> or <u>wash</u> the etchings away.

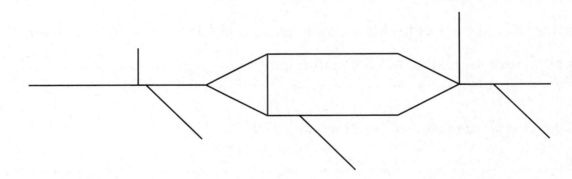

Unit 14 · Lesson 8

Exercise 4 · Use the Clues: Vocabulary Strategies

1. Work along with your teacher to use meaning cues to define quilts.

   Cummings bought a sewing machine, and it has become his companion for working on quilts—a form of art made from fabric.

2. Use meaning cues to define **mobile**.
   - Underline the vocabulary word.
   - Read the sentence aloud and look for a meaning cue.
   - Circle the meaning cue.
   - Double underline the words that define **mobile.**
   - Draw an arrow from the term **mobile** to the definition.

---

based on "Becoming an Artist"

Calder's art is known for motion. For ideas, he watched machines. "I was always delighted by the cable car. . . . The machinery and movement interested me." He studied to be a mechanical engineer. He wanted to learn to make structures and machines. Calder also imagined moving art. So he invented the mobile—a form of dangling art that swings in the air. His art is playful, and some of his biggest fans are kids. After an exhibit of his work in New York, he joked, "My fan mail is enormous; everyone is under 6."

---

3. Define the word **mobile** in your own words.

   _____

   _____

   _____

4. Verify your definition of mobile by using a dictionary or an online reference source.

Exercise 5 · Answer It: Using Signal Words

▸ Underline the signal word and answer each question.

1. What can you generalize about the artists described in this selection from reading the first sentence under each section's heading?

_____

_____

_____

2. Explain the meaning of Augusta Savage's sculpture titled *The Harp*.

_____

_____

_____

3. Explain what Alexander Calder meant when he said, "My fan mail is enormous—everyone is under 6."

_____

_____

_____

(continued)

Unit 14 · Lesson 8

4. Use a Venn diagram to show the differences between the art of Alexander Calder and Michael A. Cummings.

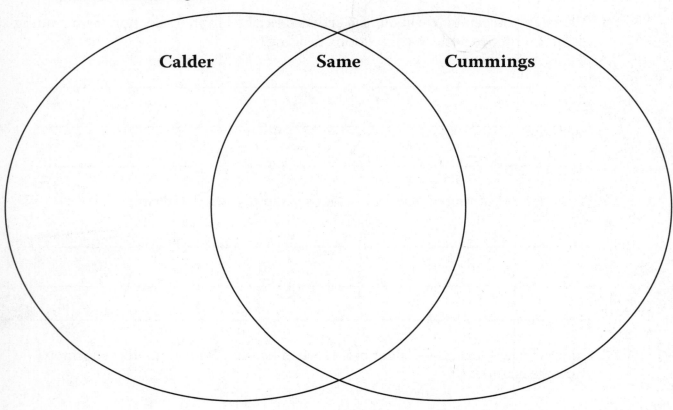

Calder   **Same**   **Cummings**

5. Classify the artists in **"Becoming an Artist"** by the type of art they created—painting, sculpture, or quilts.

Painting	Sculpture	Quilts

Exercise 1 · Listening for Stressed Syllables

▶ Listen to each word and sentence your teacher says.

▶ Repeat the word and sentence.

▶ Listen for the stressed, or accented, syllable.

▶ Put an X in the box to mark the position of the stressed syllable.

1. ☐☐

2. ☐☐

3. ☐☐

4. ☐☐

5. ☐☐

6. ☐☐

7. ☐☐

8. ☐☐

9. ☐☐

10. ☐☐

Unit 14 · Lesson 9

Exercise 2 · Build It

▸ Combine prefixes in the middle square with base words to form new words.
Example: under- + cover = undercover.

▸ Record each word in the chart below according to its prefix.

▸ Use a dictionary to verify that you are building real words.

take	arm	cover
hand	under- inter- un- in- dis-	lace
lay	mix	done

under-	inter-	un-	in-	dis-

Exercise 3 · Find It: Prefixes

▶ Read the section below.

▶ Find and underline the words with these prefixes:
under-, inter-, un-, in-, dis-, non-.

---

based on "Becoming an Artist"

Fabric Art

Michael A. Cummings' work as a quilt maker has brought him international attention. How did he become famous in this art form? A love of working with fabric underpins his success as an artist. He had been painting for twenty years, and one day he was asked to make a banner of fabric. In working on it, he discovered that this was his art form. His switch from painting to stitching quilts didn't happen in an instant. He had to buy a sewing machine and teach himself how to sew.

Now he works almost nonstop on one quilt after another. Once he finishes a quilt he disengages from it emotionally so that he can focus on the next new quilt design. People who see his quilts may be unaware of the many hours he takes to pick a theme and create a design even before he begins to sew. He draws many of his themes from Africa and the art of other African Americans.

Exercise 4 · Use the Clues: Vocabulary Strategies

▸ Work with your teacher to define the target words below.

▸ Find each boldface word below in Exercise 3: **Find It: Prefixes**, and circle it.

▸ Use the context and meaning of the prefix and base or root word to help you define the word.

▸ Write the definition on the lines below.

international— _____

_____

disengages— _____

_____

instant— _____

_____

nonstop— _____

_____

unaware— _____

_____

Exercise 5 · Revise It: Compound Subjects and Compound Predicates

▶ Read the text.

▶ Reread each pair of underlined sentences.

▶ Use a conjunction (**and/or**) to combine the subjects or predicates.

▶ Write the new sentence on the numbered line in the text below.

▶ Check for sentence signals—capital letters and end punctuation.

▶ Reread the new text together with your teacher.

---

based on "Art at Home" and "Art in Caves"

Elisa used scraps to make art. <u>Yarn can make fantastic art. Twine can make</u>
                                                                    1
<u>fantastic art.</u> <u>Nutshells became 3-D art. Caps became 3-D art.</u> Elisa's scraps
        1   2
became 3-D art in her books.

The first form of art was cave art. <u>Wind was not harmful to it. Water was</u>
                                                                        3
<u>not harmful to it.</u> Cave art tells tales of the lives of cave people. <u>The cave</u>
        3   4
<u>dwellers hunted. The cave dwellers fished.</u> <u>They sketched crude maps. They</u>
                        4   5
<u>made messages for each other.</u>
        5

Elisa used scraps to make art. _____.
                                                        1
_____. Elisa's scraps became 3-D art
                        2
in her books. The first form of art was cave art. _____
                                                                          3
_____. Cave art tells tales of the lives
of cave people. _____.
                                          4
_____
                                    5
_____.

Exercise 1 · Syllable Awareness: Segmentation

▸ Listen to each word your teacher says.

▸ Count the syllables. Write the number in the first column.

▸ Write the letter or letters for the vowel sounds you hear in each word.

▸ Say the word again. Listen for the stressed syllable.

▸ Circle the vowel sound in the stressed syllable.

	How many syllables do you hear?	First vowel sound	Second vowel sound
1.			
2.			
3.			
4.			
5.			

Exercise 2 · Match It: Homophones

▸ Read the homophones and the definitions.

▸ Draw a line to match each homophone with its definition.

▸ Use a dictionary, if necessary.

1. there
2. fir
3. your
4. they're
5. fur
6. their
7. you're
8. birth
9. berth

a. thick coat of hair
b. you + are
c. possessive form of **you**
d. place
e. evergreen tree
f. they + are
g. new life
h. possessive form of **they**
i. sleeping compartment or bunk

Check off the activities you complete with each lesson. Evaluate your accomplishments at the end of each lesson. Pay attention to teacher evaluations and comments.

	Unit Objectives (Lessons 1-5)	Lesson 1 (Date:_____)	Lesson 2 (Date:_____)
STEP 1	• Say the long vowel sounds for: **a, e, i, o,** and **u** • Identify open syllables in words.	❏ Review: Syllables ❏ Introduce: Open Syllables ❏ Phoneme Production/Replication ❏ Syllable Awareness: Segmentation	❏ Syllable Awareness: Deletion ❏ Review: Conditions for a Long Vowel Sound in an Open Syllable ❏ Vowel Chart ❏ Exercise 1: Listening for Sounds in Words
STEP 2	• Read fluently and spell words with sound spelling correspondences, syllable types, and prefixes for this and previous units. • Read fluently and spell the **Essential Words:** *good, great, right, though, through, year.*	❏ Exercise 1: Spelling Pretest 1 ❏ Memorize It	❏ Review: Syllable Types ❏ Exercise 2: Sort It: Syllable Types ❏ Word Fluency 1 ❏ Memorize It
STEP 3	• Identify synonyms, antonyms, and attributes for **Unit Words.** • Identify verbs with **-ing** endings (present participles) that act as adjectives.	❏ Explore It ❏ Expression of the Day	❏ Tense Timeline: Ongoing Action ❏ Present Participle: Suffix **-ing** ❏ Exercise 3: Find It: Present Participles ❏ Expression of the Day
STEP 4	• Identify prepositions and the meaning of prepositional phrases. • Identify and use have as a main or helping verb.	❏ Review: Noun or Adjective ❏ Exercise 2: Identify It: Noun, Adjective, or Other	❏ Review: Prepositions and Prepositional Phrases ❏ Exercise 4: Identify It: Prepositional Phrases
STEP 5	• Read phrases and passages fluently. • Preview reading selection using text features. • Define vocabulary using context-based strategies. • Read and understand informational text. • Answer multiple choice and open-ended comprehension questions. • Set a purpose, use a two-column outline, and write a concluding paragraph to prepare to write an opinion (expository) essay.	❏ Exercise 3: Phrase It ❏ Independent Text: **"Mythical Heroes"**	❏ Passage Fluency 1 ❏ Exercise 5: Find It: Open Syllables ❏ Exercise 6: Use the Clues: Vocabulary Strategies
STEP 6	• Generate sentences using a six-stage process. • Distinguish fact and opinion statements. • Answer comprehension questions beginning with **infer, identify, list, state, use, name, discuss, explain** and **describe** in complete sentences based on text. • Write an expository (opinion) essay.	❏ Masterpiece Sentences: Stages 1-3 ❏ Types of Statements: Fact or Opinion?	❏ Summarize It
	Self-Evaluation (5 is the highest) **Effort** = I produced my best work. **Participation** = I was actively involved in tasks. **Independence** = I worked on my own.	**Effort:** 1 2 3 4 5 **Participation:** 1 2 3 4 5 **Independence:** 1 2 3 4 5	**Effort:** 1 2 3 4 5 **Participation:** 1 2 3 4 5 **Independence:** 1 2 3 4 5
	Teacher Evaluation	**Effort:** 1 2 3 4 5 **Participation:** 1 2 3 4 5 **Independence:** 1 2 3 4 5	**Effort:** 1 2 3 4 5 **Participation:** 1 2 3 4 5 **Independence:** 1 2 3 4 5

Lesson 3 (Date:_____)	**Lesson 4** (Date:_____)	**Lesson 5** (Date:_____)
❑ Syllable Awareness: Deletion	❑ Exercise 1: Syllable Awareness: Segmentation	❑ Content Mastery: Syllable Awareness
❑ Exercise 1: Sort It: Syllable Types ❑ Exercise 2: Find It: Essential Words ❑ Word Fluency 1	❑ Exercise 2: Divide It ❑ Word Fluency 2 ❑ Type It: Essential Words	❑ Content Mastery: Spelling Posttest 1
❑ Exercise 3: Define It ❑ Draw It: Idioms ❑ Expression of the Day	❑ Exercise 3: Identify It: Function of -ing ❑ Expression of the Day	❑ Review: Antonyms, Synonyms, and Attributes ❑ Exercise 1: Word Relationships: Antonyms, Synonyms, and Attributes ❑ Draw It: Idioms ❑ Expression of the Day
❑ Introduce: The Verb *Have* ❑ Exercise 4: Identify It: *Have*––Main Verb or Helping Verb ❑ Exercise 5: Identify It: *Have*––Simple Verb Tenses ❑ Introduce: *Have* in Perfect Tense ❑ Exercise 6: Identify It: *Have* in Perfect Tense Verbs	❑ Exercise 4: Find It: The Helping Verb *Have* ❑ Exercise 5: Sort It: *Have* and the Perfect Tenses ❑ Exercise 6: Find It: Irregular Verbs	❑ Review: Complete Subject and Complete Predicate ❑ Masterpiece Sentences: All Stages
❑ Instructional Text: "Legendary Super Heroes" Exercise 7: Use the Clues: Vocabulary Strategies	❑ Exercise 7: Answering Multiple-Choice Comprehension Questions	❑ Prepare to Write: Expository (Opinion) Essay Exercise 2: Organize Information: Develop an Informal Outline
❑ Exercise 8: Answer It: Using Signal Words	❑ Expository (Opinion) Essay: Word Choice Exercise 8: Word Choice	❑ Organize Information: Develop an Informal Outline

Effort:	1	2	3	4	5	**Effort:**	1	2	3	4	5	**Effort:**	1	2	3	4	5
Participation:	1	2	3	4	5	**Participation:**	1	2	3	4	5	**Participation:**	1	2	3	4	5
Independence:	1	2	3	4	5	**Independence:**	1	2	3	4	5	**Independence:**	1	2	3	4	5
Effort:	1	2	3	4	5	**Effort:**	1	2	3	4	5	**Effort:**	1	2	3	4	5
Participation:	1	2	3	4	5	**Participation:**	1	2	3	4	5	**Participation:**	1	2	3	4	5
Independence:	1	2	3	4	5	**Independence:**	1	2	3	4	5	**Independence:**	1	2	3	4	5

Check off the activities you complete with each lesson. Evaluate your accomplishments at the end of each lesson. Pay attention to teacher evaluations and comments.

	Unit Objectives (Lessons 6-10)	Lesson 6 (Date:_____)	Lesson 7 (Date:_____)
STEP 1	• Say the long vowel sounds for: **a, e, i, o,** and **u** • Identify stressed syllables.	❑ Review: Stressed Syllables ❑ Exercise 1: Listening for Stressed Syllables	❑ Review: Shifting Syllable Stress ❑ Exercise 1: Listening for Stressed Syllables
STEP 2	• Read fluently and spell words with sound spelling correspondences, syllable types, and prefixes for this and previous units. • Read fluently and spell the **Essential Words:** *good, great, right, though, through, year.* • Read and spell contractions with **have.**	❑ Exercise 2: Spelling Pretest 2 ❑ Word Fluency 3	❑ Exercise 2: Divide It ❑ Exercise 3: Find It: Contractions ❑ Exercise 4: Build It: Prefixed Words
STEP 3	• Identify synonyms, antonyms, and attributes for Unit Words. • Identify verbs with -ing endings (present participles) that act as adjectives.	❑ Review: Antonyms, Synonyms, and Attributes ❑ Exercise 3: Word Relationships: Antonyms, Synonyms, and Attributes ❑ Expression of the Day	❑ Review: Prefixes ❑ Introduce: Prefixes pre-, re-, super- ❑ Exercise 5: Define It: Prefixes ❑ Expression of the Day
STEP 4	• Identify prepositions and the meaning of prepositional phrases. • Identify and use have as a main or helping verb. • Identify and write sentences with compound direct objects.	❑ Review: Conjunctions, Compound Subjects, and Compound Predicates ❑ Exercise 4: Combine It: Compound Direct Objects	❑ Review: Compound Direct Objects ❑ Exercise 6: Diagram It: Compound Direct Objects
STEP 5	• Read phrases and passages fluently. • Preview reading selection using text features. • Define vocabulary using context-based strategies. • Read and understand informational text. • Answer multiple choice and open-ended comprehension questions. • Set a purpose, use a two-column outline, and write a concluding paragraph to prepare to write an opinion (expository) essay.	❑ Exercise 5: Phrase It ❑ Independent Text: "Unsung Heroes" Exercise 6: Use the Clues: Vocabulary Strategies	❑ Passage Fluency 2 ❑ Exercise 7: Use the Clues: Vocabulary Strategies
STEP 6	• Answer comprehension questions beginning with **infer, identify, list, state, use, name, discuss, explain** and **describe** in complete sentences based on text. • Write an expository (opinion) essay. • Edit and revise an expository (opinion) essay.	❑ Exercise 7: Rewrite It: Pronouns	❑ Report Structure Exercise 8: Write It: Concluding Paragraph
	Self-Evaluation (5 is the highest) **Effort** = I produced my best work. **Participation** = I was actively involved in tasks. **Independence** = I worked on my own.	**Effort:** 1 2 3 4 5 **Participation:** 1 2 3 4 5 **Independence:** 1 2 3 4 5	**Effort:** 1 2 3 4 5 **Participation:** 1 2 3 4 5 **Independence:** 1 2 3 4 5
	Teacher Evaluation	**Effort:** 1 2 3 4 5 **Participation:** 1 2 3 4 5 **Independence:** 1 2 3 4 5	**Effort:** 1 2 3 4 5 **Participation:** 1 2 3 4 5 **Independence:** 1 2 3 4 5

Lesson 8 (Date:_____)	Lesson 9 (Date:_____)	Lesson 10 (Date:_____)
❑ Exercise 1: Listening for Word Parts	❑ Exercise 1: Listening for Stressed Syllables	❑ Exercise 1: Listening for Stressed Syllables
❑ Exercise 2: Sort It: Words Ending in o ❑ Word Fluency 4	❑ Exercise 2: Find It: Words Ending in o ❑ Exercise 3: Build It	❑ Content Mastery: Spelling Posttest 2
❑ Content Mastery: Word Relationships and Participles	❑ Exercise 4: Match It: Prefixes ❑ Expression of the Day	❑ Explore It ❑ Draw It: Idioms ❑ Expression of the Day
❑ Exercise 3: Sentence Dictation ❑ Masterpiece Sentences: Stage 2	❑ Exercise 5: Revise It: Combine Sentences with Direct Objects	❑ Content Mastery: Have—Main Verb or Helping Verb; Prepositions; and Compound Direct Object
❑ Instructional Text: "These Shoes of Mine"	❑ Exercise 6: Answering Multiple-Choice and Open-Ended Comprehension Questions	❑ Write a Concluding Paragraph for an Expository (Opinion) Essay
❑ Exercise 4: Answer It: Using Signal Words	❑ Write It: Draft Expository (Opinion) Essay	❑ Check It: Draft of an Expository (Opinion) Essay
Effort: 1 2 3 4 5 **Participation:** 1 2 3 4 5 **Independence:** 1 2 3 4 5	**Effort:** 1 2 3 4 5 **Participation:** 1 2 3 4 5 **Independence:** 1 2 3 4 5	**Effort:** 1 2 3 4 5 **Participation:** 1 2 3 4 5 **Independence:** 1 2 3 4 5
Effort: 1 2 3 4 5 **Participation:** 1 2 3 4 5 **Independence:** 1 2 3 4 5	**Effort:** 1 2 3 4 5 **Participation:** 1 2 3 4 5 **Independence:** 1 2 3 4 5	**Effort:** 1 2 3 4 5 **Participation:** 1 2 3 4 5 **Independence:** 1 2 3 4 5

Exercise 1 · Spelling Pretest 1

▸ Write the words your teacher repeats.

1. _____

2. _____

3. _____

4. _____

5. _____

6. _____

7. _____

8. _____

9. _____

10. _____

11. _____

12. _____

13. _____

14. _____

15. _____

Exercise 2 · Identify It: Noun, Adjective, or Other

▸ Read the examples with your teacher.

▸ Use the context to decide if the underlined word in the example is a noun, adjective, or another part of speech.

▸ Finish the rest of the sentences independently.

▸ Discuss the answers.

Examples:	Noun	Adjective	Other
<u>Superheroes</u> fill comic strips.	X		
Heroes have <u>superhuman</u> skills.		X	
Heroes can <u>inspire</u> us.			X

	Noun	Adjective	Other
1. Myths are made up of <u>tales</u>.			
2. <u>Early</u> people believed in myths.			
3. <u>Humans</u> wanted to understand their world.			
4. In myths, different gods <u>ruled</u> the world.			
5. <u>Romans</u> had many gods.			
6. Saturn was a <u>Roman</u> god.			
7. Juno <u>was</u> the goddess of husbands and wives.			
8. The <u>strongest</u> god was Jupiter.			
9. Neptune decided the <u>fate</u> of ships.			
10. Pluto ruled a dark and <u>gloomy</u> world.			

Exercise 3 · Phrase It

▸ Use a pencil to "scoop" the phrases in each sentence.

▸ Read each sentence as you would speak it.

▸ The first two are done for you.

1. Superheroes fill comic strips.

2. They have superhuman skills.

3. They ensure that good wins over evil.

4. Heroes can give us hope.

5. Humans wanted to make sense of their world.

6. They made up tales to explain their world.

7. These tales are called myths.

8. People lived as if myths were based in fact.

9. These myths are still told.

10. Ancient myths are intriguing.

Exercise 1 • Listening for Sounds in Words

▶ Listen to each word your teacher says.

▶ Identify the vowel sound in the first syllable of each word.

▶ Write the letter for the vowel sound and its diacritical mark on the line.

1. _____   2. _____   3. _____   4. _____   5. _____

6. _____   7. _____   8. _____   9. _____   10. _____

Exercise 2 • Sort It: Syllable Types

▶ Read the words in the **Word Bank** with your teacher.

▶ Sort the words according to their syllable type by writing each word under the correct heading.

Word Bank

corn	long	star	pen
we	press	be	or
her	me	gal	men

closed	<u>r</u>-controlled	open

Exercise 3 · Find It: Present Participles

▸ Read each sentence.

▸ Circle the present participle that acts as an adjective.

▸ Underline the noun that the present participle describes.

1. We saw the erupting volcano.

2. The ringing bell signaled a tornado.

3. Their defending champ is the hero.

4. The overlapping files were deleted.

5. Caring heroes are popular human beings.

Exercise 4 · Identify It: Prepositional Phrases

▶ Read each sentence.

▶ Reread the underlined prepositional phrase.

▶ Circle the preposition at the beginning of each phrase.

▶ Decide if the preposition shows position in space or in time.

▶ Record the preposition in the correct column.

1. In comic books, superheroes do amazing deeds.

2. Inside their dwellings, parents told children the myths.

3. Ships sailed across the sea on calm days.

4. Ships did not sail during storms.

5. Neptune was blamed when ships crashed against the rock.

6. After a storm, Neptune would calm the waves.

7. A trip into Pluto's kingdom was dark and scary.

8. Juno stood by Jupiter's side as his wife.

9. Mythical heroes ruled over the world.

10. Before scientific facts, humans believed myths to be true.

Positions in Space	Positions in Time

Exercise 5 · Find It: Open Syllables

▸ Read the text.

▸ Highlight words with **open syllables**.

▸ Sort and record the open-syllable words according to their long vowel sounds.

> **based on "Mythical Heroes"**
>
> They fill comic strips. They have superhuman skills. They're strong, quick, talented, and wise. They ensure that good wins over evil. Who are these superhumans? Superheroes! We all love heroes. Heroes can inspire us. They can give us hope. Do you have a hero?

/ $\bar{a}$ /	/ $\bar{e}$ /	/ $\bar{o}$ /	/ $\overline{oo}$ /

Exercise 6 · Use the Clues: Vocabulary Strategies

▸ Read the sentence pairs.

▸ Read the pronoun that is circled.

▸ Identify the noun that the pronoun replaces in each sentence.

▸ Underline the noun that was replaced by the pronoun.

▸ Draw an arrow to show the link between the pronoun and the noun it replaced.

▸ Refer to the Handbook section of the *Student Text* to find pronoun charts if needed.

1. Heroes can inspire us. (They) can give us hope.

2. Jupiter was the king of the gods. (He) was the strongest god.

3. Juno was his wife. (She) was the goddess of husbands and wives.

4. Neptune ruled the seas. (He) held the fate of ships in his hands.

5. It was Neptune's choice. (His) brother Pluto was ruler of the underworld.

6. Pluto ruled the underworld. (His) kingdom was a dark and gloomy land.

7. Humans wanted to make sense of their world. (They) wanted to understand its order.

8. Saturn was a Roman God. (He) was the god of time.

9. Myths are just made-up tales. People used to believe (them).

10. Ancient myths are intriguing. (They) give us insight in to the past.

Exercise 1 • Sort It: Syllable Types

▸ Read the words in the **Word Bank**.

▸ Sort the syllables in each word according to their type by writing each syllable under the correct heading.

▸ Say the syllables with your teacher.

Word Bank

acorn	equal	legal	tiger	music
debug	fever	moment	secret	silent

closed	r-controlled	open

Exercise 2 · Find It: Essential Words

▸ Write the **Essential Words** in the spaces.

_____   _____   _____

_____   _____   _____

▸ Find the **Essential Words** for this unit in these sentences.

▸ Underline them. There may be more than one in a sentence.

1. I am good at fixing equipment.

2. That was great music in the park.

3. Turn right at the next block.

4. She's only one year old though.

5. We drove through a secret tunnel.

Unit 15 · Lesson 3

Exercise 3 · Define It

▸ Define each word by filling in the blanks with a category and an attribute.

▸ Compare each definition with a dictionary definition.

▸ Do the first word with your teacher.

1. A **hero** is _____ who _____

                     category   **attribute(s)**

   _____

   _____

2. A **human** is _____ who _____

                       category   **attribute(s)**

   _____

   _____

3. A **lion** is _____ that _____

   _____

   _____

4. A **pilot** is _____ who _____

   _____

   _____

5. A **spider** is _____ that _____

   _____

   _____

6. A **tiger** is _____ that _____

   _____

   _____

(continued)

Exercise 3 (continued) · Define It

7. **Zero** is _____ that _____

_____

_____

8. **Total** is _____ that _____

_____

_____

9. **Equal** is _____ that _____

_____

_____

10. A **poem** is _____ that _____

_____

_____

Which vocabulary words are related to mammals?

▶ Write the words in the blanks.

_____   _____   _____

_____   _____

Unit 15 · Lesson 3

Exercise 4 · Identify It: *Have*—Main Verb or Helping Verb

▸ Use the **Forms of Be, Have, and Do** chart in the *Student Text* to identify the form of the verb **have** in the following sentences.

▸ Underline the form of the verb **have** in each sentence.

▸ Fill in the bubble to show if the form of **have** is used as a main verb or helping verb.

	Main Verb	Helping Verb
1. We have hope.	◯	◯
2. She has learned about myths.	◯	◯
3. He will have a vacation later.	◯	◯
4. You have passed the test.	◯	◯
5. I have been ill.	◯	◯

Exercise 5 · Identify It: *Have*—Simple Verb Tenses

▸ Use the **Helping Verb Chart** in the *Student Text* to identify the form of **have** in these sentences.

▸ Circle the verb **have** in each sentence.

▸ Fill in the bubble to show if the verb **have** is in the past, present, or future tense.

	Past	Present	Future
1. We will have lunch later.	◯	◯	◯
2. The superhero had saved the day.	◯	◯	◯
3. He has a great bike.	◯	◯	◯
4. They had chosen great music.	◯	◯	◯
5. I will have finished the project by tomorrow.	◯	◯	◯

Exercise 6 · Identify It: *Have* in Perfect Tense Verbs

▸ Circle the form of **have** in each sentence.

▸ Underline the main verb.

▸ Draw a box around the helping verb **will** if it appears in the sentence.

▸ Fill in the bubble to indicate if the verb is in the past perfect, present perfect, or future perfect tense.

	Past Perfect	Present Perfect	Future Perfect
1. Deanna has made herself a mask.	◯	◯	◯
2. She had gone to a tryout for the play.	◯	◯	◯
3. The director had given her the part of Juno.	◯	◯	◯
4. By Monday all students will have finished their costumes.	◯	◯	◯
5. Deanna has modeled her mask and costume for her family.	◯	◯	◯

Unit 15 · Lesson 3

Exercise 7 · Use the Clues: Vocabulary Strategies

1. Use substitutions to define **legends**.

   - Underline the vocabulary word.
   - Read the sentences before and after and look for a substitution.
   - Double underline the word or words you will substitute for **legends**.
   - Draw an arrow from the word **legends** to its substitution.

---

based on "Legendary Superheroes"

This isn't just the plot of an action-packed film. It's a story that's been told again and again. It's been told since people first began to entertain each other by making up stories. The stories became legends. They started as tales about real people. But as the stories were passed on for many years, they became more and more exaggerated. A fight against three people turned into a battle against ten. Eventually, there were 100 fearsome enemies! A favorite weapon became an invincible magic tool.

---

2. Define the term **legends** in your own words._____

   _____

   _____

3. Verify your definition of the term **legends** by using either an online dictionary or a print dictionary.

4. What is an example of exaggeration in the paragraph?_____

   _____

   _____

Exercise 8 · Answer It: Using Signal Words

▸ Underline the signal word and answer each question.

1. Infer what happened when Odysseus' men jumped out from hiding in the wooden horse.

_____

_____

_____

_____

_____

2. Identify the fatal flaw of two superheroes.

_____

_____

3. List the characteristics of superheroes. State whether you think everyone has what it takes to be a hero.

_____

_____

_____

_____

_____

(continued)

4. Use ideas in this text selection to create a superhero of your own. Be sure to include a name, superpowers, examples of heroic deeds, and one weakness.

_____

_____

_____

_____

5. The stories of some of these legendary superheroes come from myths. Name the mythical Greek heroes mentioned in this article. Discuss whether any of the heroes were real people.

_____

_____

_____

_____

Exercise 1 • Syllable Awareness: Segmentation

▸ Listen to the word your teacher says.

▸ Count the syllables. Write the number in the first column.

▸ Write the letter for each vowel sound you hear.

▸ Mark each short vowel with a breve (˘).

▸ Mark each long vowel with a macron (¯).

	How many syllables do you hear?	First vowel sound	Second vowel sound	Third vowel sound
1.				
2.				
3.				
4.				
5.				

Exercise 2 · Divide It

▸ Follow along with your teacher's example.

▸ Use the steps of the **Divide It Checklist** to break the words into syllables.

▸ Mark each short vowel with a breve (˘).

▸ Mark each long vowel with a macron (‾).

▸ Blend the syllables together to read the entire word.

1. music

2. donut

3. basin

4. hotel

5. unit

6. began

7. detect

8. silent

9. tiger

10. moment

Exercise 3 • Identify It: Function of -ing

▸ Read the examples with your teacher.

▸ Use context to decide if each underlined word is a present participle acting as an adjective or is part of a verb phrase indicating ongoing action.

▸ Discuss the answers.

Example:	Adjective	Part of Verb Phrase
<u>Opening</u> night was a huge success.		
He <u>is opening</u> his gifts with care.		

▸ Read the rest of the sentences independently.

▸ Decide the function of the underlined present participle.

▸ Mark the correct answer.

	Adjective	Part of Verb Phrase
1. The <u>returning</u> hero was welcomed.		
2. The hero <u>was returning</u> to his family.		
3. He is a <u>beginning</u> judo student.		
4. I <u>am beginning</u> a new class.		
5. The <u>defending</u> champ will do well.		

Unit 15 · Lesson 4

Exercise 4 · Find It: The Helping Verb *Have*

▸ Follow along with your teacher's example.

▸ Read each sentence.

▸ Underline the verb phrase and circle the form of **have**.

1. Our class (has) studied myths from all over the world.

2. By last Friday we had read three books of myths.

3. By next Wednesday we will have finished another one.

4. The myths from ancient Greece have amazed me.

5. I had enjoyed some Greek myths last year.

6. Those myths had told of Odysseus, a great hero.

7. Some people have called him the world's first superhero.

8. I have started a drawing of a great victory.

9. Odysseus has won a battle with a monster.

10. I will have completed the drawing by Sunday night.

Exercise 5 · Sort It: *Have and the Perfect Tenses*

▸ Look back at the verb phrases you underlined in Exercise 4.

▸ Write each one in the column of the chart that tells what tense it expresses.

▸ The first one has been done for you.

Past Perfect (helping verb **had**)	Present Perfect (helping verb **has** or **have**)	Future Perfect (helping verbs **will have**)
	has studied	

Exercise 6 · Find It: Irregular Verbs

▸ Read the following passage adapted from **"Mythical Heroes."**

▸ Underline each past tense form of an irregular verb.

Hint: There are ten.

> **based on "Mythical Heroes"**
>
> Early humans told myths about their world. The gods were the superheroes of the myths. They had great power.
>
> Neptune made the seas still. He held the fate of ships in his hands.
>
> Pluto was the ruler of the dark kingdom. He led the dead into the afterlife. He went into the underworld. Jupiter became the ruler of the gods. He gave orders to the other gods.

Unit 15 · Lesson 4

Exercise 7 · Answering Multiple-Choice Comprehension Questions

▸ Read each question and answer choices.

▸ Use the *Student Text* to help you choose the correct answer.

▸ Fill in the bubble for the correct answer.

1. The prefix **super-** as in the word <u>superheroes</u> means
   - Ⓐ beneath or under.
   - Ⓑ extremely small or tiny.
   - Ⓒ larger or greater than others.
   - Ⓓ again or repeatedly.

2. An antonym for the word <u>invincible</u> is
   - Ⓐ powerful.
   - Ⓑ superhuman.
   - Ⓒ weak.
   - Ⓓ tough.

3. Odysseus might be described as clever because he
   - Ⓐ used magic to move his army into Troy.
   - Ⓑ thought of a way to sneak his army into Troy.
   - Ⓒ used a magic hammer that flew back to him.
   - Ⓓ used a magic spear.

4. Which sentence from the passage most clearly helps you understand what a "fatal flaw" is?
   - Ⓐ In addition, some superheroes have a fatal flaw.
   - Ⓑ Most have one weakness that can destroy them.
   - Ⓒ With Superman, it was a mineral, kryptonite.
   - Ⓓ When Achilles was a baby, his mother dipped him in the magical river Styx.

5. The purpose of this passage is to
   - Ⓐ explain the characteristics of heroes.
   - Ⓑ tell the stories of famous heroes.
   - Ⓒ explain the quests of heroes.
   - Ⓓ discuss how all heroes use magic.

Exercise 8 · Word Choice

▶ Read these first draft paragraphs from an opinion essay. The topic for this assignment was to tell whether or not you like superheroes in movies. Below are the introductory and first body paragraphs for the assignment.

▶ Identify words or phrases that could be improved. Look for verbs, nouns, or adjectives that could be made more specific and stronger. Find at least five (5) changes you can make.

▶ Use editing marks to indicate where you would delete and add different words or phrases.

▶ Reread the paragraph using your word choice changes.

I like superheroes in movies for two reasons. Most superheroes look and live like normal people, but they do exciting things and they use their brains to get people out of dangerous situations.

Often movie superheroes don't seem to have special superhuman powers. They usually dress in shirts and ties and go to work at regular jobs. Most live in regular houses or apartments in cities. However, as soon as movie superheroes hear about someone in trouble, they put on special clothes and move fast to take care of the problem.

▶ Use a thesaurus or refer to the *Student Text* for ideas for words or information.

Antonyms

▶ Read the words in the **Word Bank**.

▶ Read each numbered word.

▶ Choose and write the word from the **Word Bank** that is an antonym (opposite) for it.

▶ Read the word pairs. Discuss your answers.

Word Bank

good	after	close
odd	remember	equal

1. before : _____

2. open : _____

3. forget : _____

4. even : _____

5. evil : _____

Synonyms

▶ Read the words in the **Word Bank**.

▶ Read each numbered word.

▶ Choose and write the word from the **Word Bank** that is a synonym (same or almost the same) for it.

▶ Read the word pairs. Discuss your answers.

(continued)

Exercise 1 (continued) · Word Relationships: Antonyms, Synonyms, and Attributes

Word Bank

equal	pupil	silent
odd	start	zero

6. none : _____

7. quiet : _____

8. same : _____

9. begin : _____

10. student : _____

Attributes

▶ Read the words in the **Word Bank**.

▶ Read each numbered word.

▶ Choose and write the word from the **Word Bank** that is an attribute of it.

▶ Read the word pairs. Discuss your answers.

Word Bank

equal	web	wind
bravery	cart	facts

11. tornado : _____

12. report : _____

13. supermarket : _____

14. hero : _____

15. spider : _____

Unit 15 · Lesson 5

Exercise 2 · Organize Information: Develop an Informal Outline

▸ Read the following prompt:

Imagine the student council at your school wants to hold an election each month for a "Hero of the Month" to acknowledge students' achievements. In addition to the honor of being elected the "Hero of the Month," the winning student will work with your principal for a day. Do you think this is a good idea? Why or why not? Write an essay in which you state your opinion on the student council's suggestion and state your reasons for the position you take.

▸ Think about the student council's suggestion. Would you be for it (pro) or against it (con)? Write your answer on the following line:

_____

_____

▸ Fill out the informal outline. Begin by choosing star ideas (reasons) for the left side of the outline, and then choose E's (examples, elaboration, and evidence) for the right side of the outline.

Topic: _____

_____

★ _____ — _____

— _____

• _____

• _____

★ _____ — _____

• _____

• _____

— _____

★ _____ — _____

• _____

• _____

— _____

(continued)

Exercise 2 (continued) · Organize Information: Develop an Informal Outline

▶ Use the outline to draft a **Two-Sentence Introductory Paragraph**.

_____

_____

_____

_____

_____

_____

Exercise 1 · Listening for Stressed Syllables

▸ Listen to each word your teacher says. Repeat the word.

▸ Listen for the stressed syllable.

▸ Make an X in the box that corresponds to the position of the stressed syllable.

	1st Syllable	2nd Syllable	3rd Syllable
1. omit			
2. minor			
3. represent			
4. elastic			
5. overly			
6. potato			
7. resulted			
8. unison			
9. indirect			
10. kimono			

Exercise 2 · Spelling Pretest 2

▶ Listen to the word your teacher repeats.

▶ Write the word.

1. _____

2. _____

3. _____

4. _____

5. _____

6. _____

7. _____

8. _____

9. _____

10. _____

11. _____

12. _____

13. _____

14. _____

15. _____

Unit 15 · Lesson 6

Exercise 3 · Word Relationships: Antonyms, Synonyms, and Attributes

▶ Read each pair of words.

▶ Sort word pairs according to their relationship by writing the word pairs in the correct columns.

▶ Discuss answers with a partner.

even : odd	deliver : transport	quiet : silent	same : equal
supermarket : cart	evil : good	tornado : wind	forget : remember
open : close	begin : start	report : facts	hero : brave

Antonyms (opposite)	Synonyms (same)	Attributes

Exercise 4 · Combine It: Compound Direct Objects

▸ Read each pair of sentences with your teacher.

▸ Underline the direct object in each sentence.

▸ Use the conjunction given to combine the two sentences into a new sentence with a compound direct object.

▸ Check for sentence signals—capital letters, commas, and end punctuation.

▸ Circle each direct object in the sentence.

1. Police find information about a crime.
   Police find evidence about crime.

or _____

2. The police arrested one suspect.
   The police did not arrest the other.

but _____

3. Some men and women join the army.
   Some join the navy.

or _____

4. Fires burn forests.
   Fires burn houses.

and _____

5. Soldiers fight the enemy.
   Soldiers do not fight friendly forces.

but _____

Unit 15 · Lesson 6

Exercise 5 · Phrase It

▸ Use the penciling strategy to "scoop" the phrases in each sentence.

▸ Read each sentence as you would speak it.

▸ The first two are done for you.

1. Unsung heroes risk their lives.

2. Firefighters are unsung heroes.

3. Men and women join the military.

4. Soldiers watch over the homelands.

5. Soldiers expect nothing in return.

6. The police are there to help.

7. Police work makes our lives safer.

8. Police help solve crimes.

9. Soldiers and firefighters are unsung heroes.

10. The police are unsung heroes.

Exercise 6 · Use the Clues: Vocabulary Strategies

▸ Read each set of sentences.

▸ Find the pronoun that is circled.

▸ Underline the noun that the pronoun replaces.

▸ Draw an arrow to show the link between the pronoun and the noun it replaced.

1. Not all heroes are superheroes. (Some) spend their lives helping others.

2. Think of firefighters. Think of soldiers. Think of the police. (These) are the unsung heroes.

3. A call to 911 is a call to save lives. (It) is your direct line to the unsung heroes.

4. Men and women join the military. (They) watch over the homelands.

5. Our soldiers expect nothing in return. We should have pride in (them)

Unit 15 · Lesson 6

Exercise 7 · Rewrite It: Pronouns

▸ Read each sentence pair in Exercise 6, **Use the Clues: Vocabulary Strategies**.

▸ Replace the circled pronoun with the noun that it represents.

▸ Rewrite the sentence using the noun.

▸ Check for sentence signals—capital letters, commas, and end punctuation.

▸ Read the new sentence.

1. _____

_____

2. _____

_____

3. _____

_____

4. _____

_____

5. _____

_____

Exercise 1 · Listening for Stressed Syllables

▸ Listen to each word your teacher says. Repeat the word.

▸ Listen for the stressed, or accented, syllable.

▸ Make an X in the box to mark the position of the stressed syllable.

1. ☐☐

2. ☐☐

3. ☐☐

4. ☐☐

5. ☐☐

6. ☐☐

7. ☐☐

8. ☐☐

9. ☐☐

10. ☐☐

Unit 15 · Lesson 7

Exercise 2 · Divide It

▸ Follow along with your teacher's example.

▸ Use the steps of **Divide It** to break the words into syllables.

▸ Blend the syllables together to read the entire word.

lion	poem	fuel
liar	prior	riot

Exercise 3 · Find It: Contractions

▸ Read each sentence.

▸ Circle the contraction in it.

▸ Expand each contraction into two words. Use the lines below.

1. They've remembered the heroes with a poem.

2. We've fed the lion a good diet.

3. I've been out of fuel.

4. You've just missed the tornadoes!

5. They get zeroes if they're late.

1. _____

2. _____

3. _____

4. _____

5. _____

Exercise 4 · Build It: Prefixed Words

▶ Read the prefixes and word parts in the box.

▶ Combine the prefixes and word parts to make new words.

▶ Record the words under the correct headings.

▶ Check a dictionary to verify that words are real words.

re-	fix	order	hero
pre-	do	fab	fine
super-	shrunk	market	turn

re-	pre-	super-

Unit 15 · Lesson 7

Exercise 5 · Define It: Prefixes

▸ Complete each sentence by writing the meaning of the underlined word.

▸ Define the prefix used in each set.

▸ Use a dictionary if you need help.

1. When you have to **redo** your homework, you have to _____.

2. When you have to **reorder** a stereo, you have to _____.

3. When you have to **return** home, you have to _____ home.

> **Re-** is a prefix that means _____
>
> _____.

4. A **prefix** is a word part that you fix, or put, _____.

5. A **prefab** house is built _____.

6. A **preshrunk** skirt is shrunk _____.

> **Pre-** is a prefix that means _____
>
> _____.

7. A **superrich** person is _____ rich.

8. A **superhero** is a hero who is _____ "ordinary" heroes.

9. A **supermarket** is a _____ where you buy food.

10. A **superfine** diamond is _____ ordinary diamonds.

> **Super-** is a prefix that means _____
>
> _____.

Exercise 6 · Diagram It: Compound Direct Objects

▶ Diagram the first sentence in the exercise with your teacher.

▶ Diagram the remaining compound direct object sentences independently.

▶ Write an X above the vertical line that separates the complete subject and the complete predicate.

1. Police stop crime and misconduct.

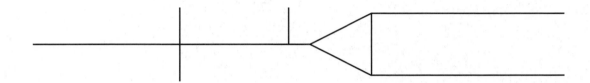

2. The police enforce traffic rules and safety regulations.

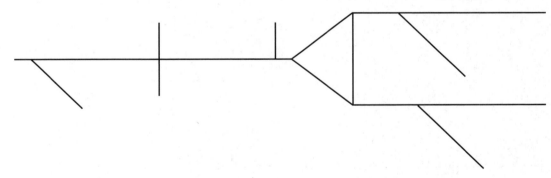

(continued)

3. Forest rangers monitor national parks and remote areas for fires.

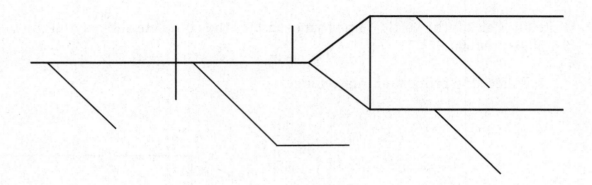

4. They relay messages or information to firefighters.

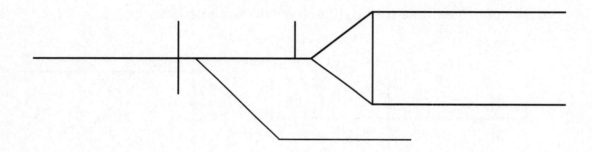

5. Soldiers also defend our country and its people.

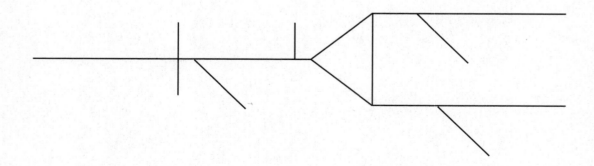

▸ Read the passage.

▸ Read the circled pronouns.

▸ Underline the noun that the pronoun replaces.

▸ Draw an arrow to the word(s) it represents.

---

based on "Unsung Heroes"

Crime is a big problem. (It) is everywhere. Some people shoplift. Some
1
use drugs. Some are reckless drivers. Some harm others. The police
are there to help. (They) bring back order. (They) help solve crimes.
2 3
(Their) work makes our lives safer. Like soldiers and firefighters, (they)
4 5
are unsung heroes.
5

Unit 15 · Lesson 7

Exercise 8 · Write It: Concluding Paragraph

▸ Read each introductory paragraph and concluding paragraph.

▸ Find the call to action in the concluding paragraph and underline it.

▸ Decide what the author is asking you to do and write it in the space provided.

1. **Introductory paragraph:** There are many jobs in the world that require people to be heroes every day. I would like to be a firefighter so that I could protect people from fires.

   Concluding paragraph: Firefighters work every day to protect us. Firefighters aren't the only people who can help our community. We can help by being careful with fire when we cook, camp, or use our fireplaces.

   What does the author want you to do? _____

   _____

2. **Introductory paragraph:** Many people think of heroes as people with magic powers. Not every hero has a superpower.

   Concluding paragraph: Everyone can be a hero. There are always chances to be a hero at home. You can help your friends and family every day if you use your mind and your heart as your superpower.

   What does the author want you to do? _____

   _____

3. **Introductory paragraph:** There are many reasons I would like to be a superhero. I would have superpowers, save people from danger, and protect innocent people.

   Concluding paragraph: It would be great to be a superhero. Just because you aren't a superhero doesn't mean you can't be a hero. Think about how you can help people. You will see that there are many ways you can be a hero to people you know.

   What does the author want you to do? _____

   _____

Exercise 1 · Listening for Word Parts

▸ Listen to each word your teacher says.

▸ Mark **Yes** or **No** to show whether or not the word has a suffix.

▸ If **Yes**, write the suffix.

	Do you hear a suffix on the word?		If **Yes**, what is the suffix?
	Yes	No	
1.			
2.			
3.			
4.			
5.			
6.			
7.			
8.			
9.			
10.			

Unit 15 · Lesson 8

Exercise 2 · Sort It: Words Ending in o

▶ Read the words in the **Word Bank**.

▶ Sort the words according to a spelling or syllable pattern.

  Hint: Notice what comes before the final **o** in each word.

▶ Label the headings.

Word Bank

heroes	tornadoes	videos	stereos
radios	cargoes	potatoes	goes

Exercise 3 · Sentence Dictation

▸ Write the sentences that your teacher dictates.

▸ Check for sentence signals—correct capitalization and end punctuation.

▸ Choose one sentence for use with the next activity, **Masterpiece Sentences**.

1. _____

2. _____

3. _____

4. _____

5. _____

Exercise 4 · Answer It: Using Signal Words

▸ Underline the signal words in each question and write the answers in complete sentences.

▸ Check for sentence signals—capital letters, commas, and end punctuation.

1. Use drawings to show the expression of Manuel's mood change from the beginning to the end of the story. Then explain the mood change in words.

_____

_____

_____

_____

_____

(continued)

2. Describe Manuel's feeling for his mother.

_____

_____

_____

_____

3. Discuss whether Manuel is a hero at the end of the story.

_____

_____

_____

4. Infer what Manuel learned by giving his shoes to his uncle.

_____

_____

_____

_____

5. **"These Shoes of Mine"** is a drama. Explain how this type of writing is different from a story such as **"Podway Bound"** in Unit 13. Explain whether you think a play is easier or harder to read.

_____

_____

_____

_____

_____

Exercise 1 · Listening for Stressed Syllables

▸ Listen to each word your teacher says. Repeat the word.

▸ Listen for the stressed syllable.

▸ Place an X in the box to mark the position of the stressed syllable.

	1st Syllable	2nd Syllable	3rd Syllable	4th Syllable
1. condo				
2. super				
3. remember				
4. respect				
5. reordering				
6. driver				
7. reviving				
8. paper				
9. republic				
10. stucco				

Unit 15 · Lesson 9

Exercise 2 · Find It: Words Ending in o

▸ Use your Spelling Lists from Lessons 6–10 in the *Student Text* to find words whose singular form ends with **o**.

▸ Write the singular form in the first column.

▸ Add **-s** or **-es** to each word. Write the new words in the second column.

Hint: One word doesn't follow the rule. Use a dictionary to discover which word is an exception to the spelling rule.

▸ Circle the exception to the spelling rule.

1. _____   _____

2. _____   _____

3. _____   _____

Exercise 3 · Build It

▶ Combine prefixes in the middle square with word parts to form new words.

Example: re + charge = recharge.

▶ Record each new word in the chart according to its prefix.

▶ Use a dictionary to verify that you are building real words.

vise	pay	state
ject	inter- in- re- dis- super- pre-	cline
scribe	fer	charge

inter-	in-	re-	dis-	super-	pre-

Unit 15 • Lesson 9

Exercise 4 • Match It: Prefixes

▸ Read each prefix in the first column.

▸ Find its definition in the second column.

▸ Draw a line to connect the prefix with its definition.

1. un-		back, again
2. re-		into
3. pre-		above, beyond, bigger
4. super-		not
5. in-		before

▸ Follow the same procedure with these prefixes and definitions.

6. inter-		not
7. under-		below
8. non-		between
9. dis-		away, apart

Exercise 5 · Revise it: Combine Sentences with Direct Objects

▶ Read the text.

▶ Reread the underlined sentences.

▶ Use a conjunction (and/or/but) to combine each pair of sentences into a single sentence with a compound direct object.

▶ Write the new sentence on the corresponding numbered line in the text below.

▶ Reread the new text together with your teacher.

---

based on "Unsung Heroes"

Fire can be a big problem. <u>Fires burn homes. Fires burn trees on</u>
<u>huge plots of land.</u> <u>Firefighters save lives. Firefighters save property.</u>
Firefighters are unsung heroes.

The military protects our homeland. <u>Men and women join the army.</u>
<u>Men and women join the navy.</u>

<u>Our soldiers and sailors deserve our thanks. Our soldiers and sailors</u>
<u>deserve our gratitude.</u>

<u>We should have pride in them. We should have confidence in them.</u>
People in the military are also unsung heroes.

Fire is a big problem. _____.

_____. Firefighters are unsung heroes.

The military protects our homeland. _____

_____

_____

People in the military are also unsung heroes.

Exercise 6 · Answering Multiple-Choice and Open-Ended Comprehension Questions

▸ Read the following selection. Then, use the selection to answer the questions on the following page.

*Eskimos: Land and People

What do you know of the Eskimos' land? It is vast. It crosses Asia and North America. Much of the land is permanently frozen. It is often windy. Most of it is treeless. Yet the Eskimos call it the "Beautiful Land." This land has been their home for thousands of years.

The seasons bring different challenges to the Eskimo people. In winter, temperatures fall below 0°F. Sometimes, they dip below -80°F. For months, the sun never rises above the horizon. There are just a few hours of light each day. In contrast, summers are short. Summer temperatures can rise to around 80°F. Daylight lasts up to 24 hours. Bogs and swamps dot the land. Many Eskimos use the summer months to hunt and gather food for the winter.

Modern inventions have brought changes to the old way of life. Snowmobiles are replacing dog sleds. Metal is replacing bone and stone tools. Television is replacing storytelling. Some Eskimos worry these changes will erase the Eskimo culture. Grandparents teach the children. They teach the stories and traditions of their ancestors. They teach the Eskimo languages. They practice the old arts and crafts. They encourage the children to respect the ways of the past.

*Eskimos are known today by several names: "Eskimo" or "Inuit" (Alaska); "Inuit" (Canada); "Kalaadit" (Greenland)

(continued)

Exercise 6 (continued) · Answering Multiple-Choice and Open-Ended Comprehension Questions

▸ Read each question and answer choices.

▸ Fill in the bubble for the correct answer.

1. We know from the first paragraph that the land of the Eskimos
- Ⓐ is usually warm.
- Ⓑ has many trees.
- Ⓒ has few trees.
- Ⓓ has little wind.

2. An antonym for the word <u>vast</u> in the second sentence is
- Ⓐ small.
- Ⓑ sunny.
- Ⓒ huge.
- Ⓓ cold.

3. The Eskimos
- Ⓐ are used to many hours of sunlight during the winter.
- Ⓑ don't have much sunlight in the summer.
- Ⓒ enjoy long, warm summers.
- Ⓓ are used to very cold weather in the winter.

4. To make sure that they have enough to eat, many Eskimos
- Ⓐ use the short winters to hunt and gather food.
- Ⓑ always shop at grocery stores.
- Ⓒ use the short summers to find enough food for the winter.
- Ⓓ probably send their grandparents to buy food.

5. We know from the last paragraph that some Eskimos are concerned that
- Ⓐ the long summers are too warm.
- Ⓑ their culture will disappear.
- Ⓒ there are not enough cold days.
- Ⓓ there is too much daylight in the winter.

(continued)

Exercise 6 (continued) · Answering Multiple-Choice and Open-Ended Comprehension Questions

6. What can you generalize about life as an Eskimo during the winter? Use the text selection to help with your answer.

_____

_____

_____

_____

_____

_____

_____

_____

_____

Trait	Point
Ideas/Content	
Organization	
Word Choice	
Sentence Fluency	
Conventions	

Total Number Correct _____ /10

Exercise 1 · Listening for Stressed Syllables

▶ Listen to each word your teacher says.

▶ Count the syllables. Write the number in the first column.

▶ Say the word again. Listen for the stressed syllable.

▶ Write the letters for the stressed syllable in the correct column.

	How many syllables do you hear?	First Syllable	Second Syllable	Third Syllable
1.				
2.				
3.				
4.				
5.				
6.				
7.				
8.				
9				
10.				

Check off the activities you complete with each lesson. Evaluate your accomplishments at the end of each lesson. Pay attention to teacher evaluations and comments.

	Unit Objectives (Lessons 1-5)	Lesson 1 (Date:_____)	Lesson 2 (Date:_____)
STEP 1	• Practice syllable segmentation and identify stressed syllables in multisyllable words. • Identify final silent **e** syllables in words. • Identify vowel phonemes.	❑ Review: Vowels and Consonants ❑ Review: Final Silent **e** Syllable ❑ Phoneme Production/Replication ❑ Listening for Sounds in Words	❑ Review: Conditions for Long Vowel Sounds ❑ Introduce: Conditions for Final Silent **e** in Two-Syllable Words ❑ Exercise 1: Listening for Sounds in Words
STEP 2	• Read fluently and spell words with sound spelling correspondences, syllable types, and prefixes for this and previous units. • Read fluently and spell the **Essential Words**: *again, sound, today, tomorrow, want, work.*	❑ Exercise 1: Spelling Pretest 1 ❑ Handwriting Practice: Timed ❑ Memorize It	❑ Review: Syllable Types ❑ Exercise 2: Sort It: Syllable Types ❑ Word Fluency 1 ❑ Memorize It ❑ Handwriting Practice
STEP 3	• Use synonyms, antonyms, and attribute relationships to define **Unit Words**. • Identify past and present participles used as adjectives.	❑ Explore It ❑ Expression of the Day	❑ Introduce: Past Participles ❑ Exercise 3: Find It: Past Participles ❑ Expression of the Day
STEP 4	• Identify plural and possessive noun forms. • Identify prepositions and prepositional phrases. • Identify and use the verbs **be** and **have**.	❑ Review: Possessive Nouns ❑ Exercise 2: Identify It: Plural or Possessive ❑ Review: Possessive Pronouns ❑ Exercise 3: Find It: Possessives	❑ Review: Prepositions and Prepositional Phrases ❑ Exercise 4: Find It: Prepositional Phrases ❑ Review: Object of the Preposition ❑ Exercise 5: Identify It: Object of the Preposition
STEP 5	• Read phrases and passages fluently. • Preview nonfciton reading selection using text features. • Define vocabulary using context-based strategies. • Read and understand informational text. • Review components, label parts of a business letter.	❑ Exercise 4: Phrase It ❑ Independent Text: **"The Complete Athlete"**	❑ Exercise 6: Find It: Words with Final Silent **e** ❑ Passage Fluency 1 ❑ Exercise 7: Use the Clues: Vocabulary Strategies
STEP 6	• Generate sentences using a six-stage process. • Distinguish fact and opinion statements. • Answer comprehension questions using **describe, use, infer, explain, select, distinguish**, and **tell**. • Write a business letter.	❑ Masterpiece Sentences: Stages 1–3 ❑ Sentence Types: Fact or Opinion?	❑ Introduce: Types of Letters —Informal and Business ❑ Letter Writing Format: Informal or Business Exercise 8: Letters: Informal or Business
	Self-Evaluation (5 is the highest) **Effort** = I produced my best work. **Participation** = I was actively involved in tasks. **Independence** = I worked on my own.	**Effort:** 1 2 3 4 5 **Participation:** 1 2 3 4 5 **Independence:** 1 2 3 4 5	**Effort:** 1 2 3 4 5 **Participation:** 1 2 3 4 5 **Independence:** 1 2 3 4 5
	Teacher Evaluation	**Effort:** 1 2 3 4 5 **Participation:** 1 2 3 4 5 **Independence:** 1 2 3 4 5	**Effort:** 1 2 3 4 5 **Participation:** 1 2 3 4 5 **Independence:** 1 2 3 4 5

Lesson 3 (Date:_____)	**Lesson 4** (Date:_____)	**Lesson 5** (Date:_____)
❑ Phoneme Segmentation ❑ Phoneme Substitution ❑ Syllable Awareness: Segmentation ❑ Exercise 1: Listening for Sounds in Words	❑ Exercise 1: Syllable Awareness: Segmentation	❑ Content Mastery: Syllable Awareness
❑ Exercise 2: Divide It ❑ Exercise 3: Find It: Essential Words ❑ Word Fluency 1	❑ Review: Drop **e** Rule ❑ Drop It: Drop **e** Rule ❑ Word Fluency 2 ❑ Type It: Essential Words	❑ Content Mastery: Spelling Posttest 1
❑ Exercise 4: Define It ❑ Draw It: Idioms ❑ Expression of the Day	❑ Introduce: Prefix: **sub-** ❑ Exercise 2: Define It: Prefixed Words ❑ Exercise 3: Identify It: Suffixes **-ed** and **-en** ❑ Expression of the Day	❑ Review: Word Relationships: Antonyms, Synonyms, and Attributes ❑ Exercise 1: Word Relationships: Antonyms, Synonyms, and Attributes ❑ Draw It: Idioms ❑ Expression of the Day
❑ Review: The Verbs **Be**, **Have** ❑ Exercise 5: Identify It: Main Verb or Helping Verb	❑ Review: Irregular Verbs ❑ Exercise 4: Rewrite It: Past Forms of Irregular Verbs ❑ Exercise 5: Find It: Past Forms of Irregular Verbs	❑ Masterpiece Sentences: Stage 4: Paint Your Subject
❑ Instructional Text: **"Tony Hawk: Extreme Athlete"** Exercise 6: Use the Clues	❑ Review: Business Letters	❑ Review: Business Letter
❑ Exercise 7: Answer It: Using Signal Words	❑ Write It: Business Letter Exercise 6: Writing Business Letters	❑ Prepare to Write: Business Letter Exercise 2: Writing Business Letters

Effort:	1	2	3	4	5	**Effort:**	1 2 3 4 5		**Effort:**	1	2	3	4	5
Participation:	1	2	3	4	5	**Participation:**	1 2 3 4 5		**Participation:**	1	2	3	4	5
Independence:	1	2	3	4	5	**Independence:**	1 2 3 4 5		**Independence:**	1	2	3	4	5

Effort:	1	2	3	4	5	**Effort:**	1 2 3 4 5		**Effort:**	1	2	3	4	5
Participation:	1	2	3	4	5	**Participation:**	1 2 3 4 5		**Participation:**	1	2	3	4	5
Independence:	1	2	3	4	5	**Independence:**	1 2 3 4 5		**Independence:**	1	2	3	4	5

Check off the activities you complete with each lesson. Evaluate your accomplishments at the end of each lesson. Pay attention to teacher evaluations and comments.

	Unit Objectives (Lessons 6-10)	Lesson 6 (Date:_____)	Lesson 7 (Date:_____)
STEP 1	• Practice syllable segmentation and identify stressed syllables in multisyllable words. • Identify final silent **e** syllables in words. • Identify vowel phonemes.	❑ Review: Schwa ❑ Exercise 1: Listening for Stressed Syllables	❑ Exercise 1: Listening for Word Parts ❑ Exercise 2: Listening for Stressed Syllables
STEP 2	• Read fluently and spell words with sound spelling correspondences, syllable types, and prefixes for this and previous units. • Read fluently and spell the **Essential Words**: *again, sound, today, tomorrow, want, work*. • Read and spell contractions with **had** and **has**.	❑ Exercise 2: Spelling Pretest 2 ❑ Word Fluency 3 ❑ Handwriting Practice: Timed	❑ Exercise 3: Divide It ❑ Exercise 4: Find It: Contractions ❑ Word Fluency 4
STEP 3	• Use synonyms, antonyms, and attribute relationships to define **Unit Words**. • Identify past and present participles used as adjectives.	❑ Review: Antonyms, Synonyms, and Attributes ❑ Introduce: Analogies ❑ Exercise 3: Word Relationships: Analogies ❑ Expression of the Day	❑ Review: Verb Endings ❑ Review: Past Participles ❑ Exercise 5: Find It: Present and Past Participles as Adjectives ❑ Introduce: Participial Phrases with Past Participles ❑ Exercise 6: Find It: Participial Phrases with Past Participles
STEP 4	• Identify plural and possessive noun forms. • Identify prepositions and prepositional phrases. • Identify and use the verbs **be** and **have**. • Identify adjectives of the same kind in sentences.	❑ Introduce: Adjectives of the Same Kind ❑ Exercise 4: Find It: Adjectives of the Same Kind	❑ Review: Adjectives of the Same Kind ❑ Exercise 7: Diagram It: Adjectives of the Same Kind
STEP 5	• Read phrases and passages fluently. • Preview nonfiction reading selection using text features. • Define vocabulary using context-based strategies. • Read and understand informational text. • Review components, label parts of a business letter.	❑ Exercise 5: Phrase It ❑ Independent Text: **"Extreme Athletes"** Exercise 6: Use the Clues: Vocabulary Strategies	❑ Passage Fluency 2
STEP 6	• Answer comprehension questions using **describe, use, infer, explain, select, distinguish,** and **tell**. • Write an expository essay using a two-column outline, and including an introductory paragraph, body paragraphs, and concluding paragraph. • Edit and revise an expository essay.	❑ Exercise 7: Rewrite It: Pronouns	❑ Prepare to Write: Expository Essay Exercise 8: Organizing Information: Informal Outline
	Self-Evaluation (5 is the highest) **Effort** = I produced my best work. **Participation** = I was actively involved in tasks. **Independence** = I worked on my own.	**Effort:** 1 2 3 4 5 **Participation:** 1 2 3 4 5 **Independence:** 1 2 3 4 5	**Effort:** 1 2 3 4 5 **Participation:** 1 2 3 4 5 **Independence:** 1 2 3 4 5
	Teacher Evaluation	**Effort:** 1 2 3 4 5 **Participation:** 1 2 3 4 5 **Independence:** 1 2 3 4 5	**Effort:** 1 2 3 4 5 **Participation:** 1 2 3 4 5 **Independence:** 1 2 3 4 5

Lesson 8 (Date:_____)	**Lesson 9** (Date:_____)	**Lesson 10** (Date:_____)
❏ Exercise 1: Listening for Word Parts	❏ Exercise 1: Listening for Stressed Syllables	❏ Exercise 1: Listening for Stressed Syllables
❏ Review: The Role of **e** ❏ Drop It ❏ Word Fluency 4	❏ Exercise 2: Build It	❏ Content Mastery: Spelling Posttest 2
❏ Content Mastery: Word Relationships and Past Participles Used as Adjectives	❏ Introduce: Prefix **anti-** ❏ Exercise 3: Define It ❏ Expression of the Day	❏ Explore It: Athlete ❏ Draw It: Idioms ❏ Expression of the Day
❏ Masterpiece Sentences: All Stages ❏ Rewrite It: Adjectives of the Same Kind	❏ Review: Object of the Preposition ❏ Exercise 4: Find It: Object of the Preposition ❏ Exercise 5: Find It: Adjectives of the Same Kind	❏ Content Mastery: Plural and Possessive Nouns; Prepositional Phrases; Adjectives of the Same Kind
❏ Instructional Text: **"A Special Kind of Athlete"** Exercise 2: Use the Clues	❏ Review Content and Ideas for an Expository Essay	❏ Oral Presentation of Expository Essays
❏ Exercise 3: Answer It: Using Signal Words	❏ Write It: Expository Essay	❏ Check It: Draft of an Expository Essay
Effort: 1 2 3 4 5 **Participation:** 1 2 3 4 5 **Independence:** 1 2 3 4 5	**Effort:** 1 2 3 4 5 **Participation:** 1 2 3 4 5 **Independence:** 1 2 3 4 5	**Effort:** 1 2 3 4 5 **Participation:** 1 2 3 4 5 **Independence:** 1 2 3 4 5
Effort: 1 2 3 4 5 **Participation:** 1 2 3 4 5 **Independence:** 1 2 3 4 5	**Effort:** 1 2 3 4 5 **Participation:** 1 2 3 4 5 **Independence:** 1 2 3 4 5	**Effort:** 1 2 3 4 5 **Participation:** 1 2 3 4 5 **Independence:** 1 2 3 4 5

Exercise 1 · Spelling Pretest 1

▶ Write each word your teacher repeats.

1. _____	6. _____	11. _____
2. _____	7. _____	12. _____
3. _____	8. _____	13. _____
4. _____	9. _____	14. _____
5. _____	10. _____	15. _____

Exercise 2 · Identify It: Plural or Possessive

▶ Read each sentence.

▶ Decide if the underlined word is a plural noun, a singular possessive noun, or a plural possessive noun.

▶ Fill in the correct bubble.

	Plural Noun	Singular Possessive	Plural Possessive
1. <u>Fabiola's</u> desire to win is impressive.	◯	◯	◯
2. Extreme sports test <u>athletes'</u> skills.	◯	◯	◯
3. Extreme <u>skaters'</u> skates are a new type.	◯	◯	◯
4. Extreme skaters have their own <u>parks</u>.	◯	◯	◯
5. That <u>skater's</u> helmet protects her.	◯	◯	◯

Exercise 3 · Find It: Possessives

▸ Read each sentence.

▸ Find the possessive pronoun.

▸ Underline the possessive pronoun if it is used like an adjective before a noun.

▸ Circle the possessive pronoun if it is used alone.

1. Skate parks in our city have big ramps.

2. We call the park by the school ours.

3. Mark and his brother skate there.

4. These pads must be theirs.

5. I know these skates are yours.

6. Tina and her friends can do bashing.

7. Mark showed us his new trick.

8. The park has its hours posted.

9. The green helmet is mine.

10. I asked the twins if these skate bags were theirs.

Exercise 4 · Phrase It

▸ Read the sentences as you would speak them.

▸ Use the penciling strategy to "scoop" the phrases in each sentence.

▸ The first two are done for you as examples.

1. One person can make things happen.

2. Shriver began a summer day camp.

3. The camp was for athletes.

4. She held the camp at her home.

5. She invited kids like Steven.

6. She watched them compete in sports.

7. Shriver saw them smile.

8. Athletes come to play in the games.

9. These athletes compete at no cost.

10. Help fund Special Olympics!

Exercise 1 · Listening for Sounds in Words

▸ Listen to each word your teacher says.

▸ Decide where the long vowel sound occurs in the word.

▸ Circle the position of the long vowel sound:
B for beginning, **M** for middle, and **E** for end.

1. B   M   E

2. B   M   E

3. B   M   E

4. B   M   E

5. B   M   E

6. B   M   E

7. B   M   E

8. B   M   E

9. B   M   E

10. B   M   E

Exercise 2 · Sort It: Syllable Types

▸ Read the words in the **Word Bank**.

▸ Sort each word according to its syllable type by writing the word under the correct heading.

Word Bank

fine	ate	she	came
back	side	pass	we
be	fig	hand	he

closed	final silent -e	open

Exercise 3 · Find It: Past Participles

▸ Each sentence contains a past participle ending in **-ed** or **-en**.

▸ Read each sentence.

▸ Underline the past participle and the noun that it describes or modifies.

▸ Answer the question about the noun.

▸ Use the examples as models.

Part A

Sentence	What kind? or Which one?
Example: Broken glass fell from the ornate frame.	What kind of glass? broken
Example: The undercover cops observe the deserted apartment.	What kind of apartment? deserted
1. Chen will ask the uninvited visitors to depart.	Which visitors?
2. Shattered glass ruined the front tires of Pedro's car.	What kind of glass?
3. The pampered child whined all day.	Which child?
4. Lu and Chen discover the misfiled papers just in time for class.	What papers?
5. Before the game, Ramon was named the designated hitter.	What kind of hitter?

(continued)

Exercise 3 (continued) · Find It: Past Participles

Part B

Use the underlined past participles from **Part A** to complete the activities.

6. Complete the antonym pair:

   invited: _____

7. Complete the synonym pair:

   spoiled: _____

8. Complete this sentence.

   The runners get water at _____ spots along the race route.

9. Define the word **misfile**:

   _____

10. Choose two of the part participles you underlined and use them in sentences. Make sure the past participle in each sentence does the job of an adjective.

    _____

    _____

Exercise 4 · Find It: Prepositional Phrases

▸ Read each sentence.

▸ Find and underline each prepositional phrase in it.

▸ Circle the preposition.

▸ Then put a square around the object of the preposition.

1. Tony Hawk had a sponsor at 12.

2. He became the best skateboarder in the world.

3. In most contests, he was the winner.

4. He bought two homes with his winnings.

5. Then the years of financial success ended.

Exercise 5 · Identify It: Object of the Preposition

▸ Read each sentence.

▸ Decide if the underlined noun in each sentence functions as a direct object or as an object of a preposition.

▸ Fill in the bubble to mark the answer.

	Direct Object	Object of Preposition
1. Tony Hawk had <u>problems</u> with money.	◯	◯
2. He started a company with another <u>skateboarder</u>.	◯	◯
3. The company did not make money for its <u>owners</u>.	◯	◯
4. Then skateboarding made a <u>comeback</u>.	◯	◯
5. Companies offered big money to <u>skateboarders</u>.	◯	◯

Unit 16 · Lesson 2

Exercise 6 · Find It: Words with Final Silent e

▸ Read the excerpt from **"The Complete Athlete."**

▸ Highlight or underline words with **final silent e**.

▸ Sort the words according to their long vowel sound.

> **based on "The Complete Athlete"**
>
> Now, Special Olympics is important in the lives of many people.
> Today, there are 27 sports. There are summer and winter sports.
> From all over the world, athletes come to play in the games.
> These athletes compete at no cost. How are the games funded?
> Shriver has used grants. Many have donated. Many others have
> made money with events. You can help, too. Get started! Help fund
> Special Olympics!

$\bar{a}$	$\bar{e}$	$\bar{\imath}$	$\bar{o}$	$\overline{oo}$

Exercise 7 · Use the Clues: Vocabulary Strategies

▸ Read the sentence pairs.

▸ Read the pronoun that is circled.

▸ Identify the noun that the circled pronoun replaces in each sentence.

▸ Draw an arrow to show the link between the pronoun and the noun it replaces.

▸ Underline the noun that was replaced by the pronoun.

1. Mark loves sports. (He) is not like other athletes.

2. There are many like Mark and Kate. Yes, (their) skills are limited.

3. Shriver began a summer day camp. (She) held the camp at her home.

4. She invited kids like Mark and Kate. She watched (them) compete in sports.

5. From all over the world, athletes come to play in the games. (They) compete at no cost.

Unit 16 · Lesson 2

Exercise 8 · Letters: Informal or Business

▶ Read each prompt and decide whether the letter is an informal letter or a business letter. Put a check in the correct box to indicate your choice.

▶ Explain how you decided which type of letter you would write. Write your explanation on the lines.

1. Write a thank you note to your Aunt Yolanda. Her contact information is Yolanda Jones, 222 Tomorrow St., Monday, CA 93939.

❏ Informal letter   ❏ Business letter

How did you decide the type of letter?

_____

_____

_____

_____

2. Write a letter asking the Sunnyday Humane Society to speak at a school assembly about volunteering opportunities. Their contact information is 4545 E. 1st St., Sunnyday, FL 33333.

❏ Informal letter   ❏ Business letter

How did you decide the type of letter?

_____

_____

_____

_____

(continued)

Exercise 8 (continued) · Letters: Informal or Business

3. Write a letter to the company called Mytown Mail Order, Inc. about the condition of the electronics equipment you ordered, which arrived damaged. Their contact information is 8342 Main St., Mytown, OH 43475.

❑ Informal letter   ❑ Business letter

How did you decide the type of letter?

_____

_____

_____

4. Write a letter to a local nursery asking whether they will donate plants to be used for a new garden at your school. Their contact information is The Readingtown Garden Center, 9700 Ash St., Readingtown, TX 77777.

❑ Informal letter   ❑ Business letter

How did you decide the type of letter?

_____

_____

_____

5. Write a letter to your grandmother, who lives out of town, asking when she is coming for her next visit. Her contact information is Emma Smith (or use your own grandmother's name) 5530 Wren Ave., Writetown, NY 11011.

❑ Informal letter   ❑ Business letter

How did you decide the type of letter?

_____

_____

_____

Exercise 1 · Listening for Sounds in Words

▸ Listen to each word your teacher says.

▸ Put an X in the column to indicate the long vowel sound you hear.

	$\bar{a}$	$\bar{e}$	$\bar{\imath}$	$\bar{o}$	$\overline{oo}$
1.					
2.					
3.					
4.					
5.					
6.					
7.					
8.					
9.					
10.					

Exercise 2 · Divide It

▸ Read each sentence silently.

▸ Use the steps of **Divide It** to break each **boldface** word into syllables.

▸ Blend the syllables together to read each boldface word.

▸ After dividing both boldface words, read the sentence to a partner.

1. The **athletes compete** in contests.

   athletes   compete

2. **Extreme** sports **require** pads and helmets.

   extreme   require

3. **Competitors** don't want to **injure** themselves.

   competitors   injure

Unit 16 · Lesson 3

Exercise 3 · Find It: Essential Words

▶ Write the **Essential Words** in the spaces.

_____ _____ _____

_____ _____ _____

▶ Find the **Essential Words** for this unit in these sentences.

▶ Underline them. There may be more than one in a sentence.

1. Tomorrow, we are going to compete again.

2. Today is a day for practice.

3. I want to take my game to a new level.

4. I will work hard on my tricks.

5. Start when you hear this sound.

Exercise 4 · Define It

▸ Complete each definition by filling in the blanks with a category and one or more attributes.

▸ Compare any definition that you're unsure of with a dictionary definition.

▸ Do the first word with your teacher.

1. An **athlete** is a(n) _____ who _____
                  category   **attribute(s)**

   _____

   _____ .

2. **Brave** is a(n) _____ that _____
               category   **attribute(s)**

   _____

   _____ .

3. A **game** is a(n) _____ that _____

   _____

   _____ .

4. A **backbone** is a(n) _____ that _____

   _____

   _____ .

5. **Compete** is a(n) _____ that _____

   _____

   _____ .

6. A **candidate** is a(n) _____ who _____

   _____

   _____ .

7. A **hurricane** is a(n) _____ that _____

   _____

   _____ .

(continued)

Exercise 4 (continued) · Define It

8. **Climate** is a(n) _____ that _____

_____

_____ .

9. A **trombone** is a(n) _____ that _____

_____

_____ .

10. A **minute** is a(n) _____ that _____

_____

_____ .

Which vocabulary words are related to **athletes**?

▸ Write the words in the blanks.

_____   _____   _____

_____   _____   _____

Exercise 5 · Identify It: Main Verb or Helping Verb

▶ Read each sentence with your teacher.

▶ Underline the verb or verb phrase.

▶ Decide if the form of **be** or **have** is used as a main verb or a helping verb.

▶ Fill in the correct bubble.

▶ Do the first sentence with your teacher.

	Main Verb	Helping Verb
1. The athlete has waited an hour.	○	○
2. We were prepared for the long and hot game.	○	○
3. She is a strong and energetic leader.	○	○
4. Our team has scored many difficult points.	○	○
5. At last, we were victorious.	○	○
6. There will be an extreme sports competition this winter.	○	○
7. Next year our team will have even more well-trained and competitive athletes.	○	○
8. Mark has tried many different sports.	○	○
9. The scoreboard was flashing the winning time.	○	○
10. Mark has four gold medals.	○	○

Unit 16 · Lesson 3

Exercise 6 · Use the Clues: Vocabulary Strategies

1. Use meaning cues along with your teacher to define **coping**.

Take the metal bar at the top of the ramp where they do tricks. It has a name. It's the "coping."

2. Use meaning cues to define **retire**.
    - Underline the term.
    - Read the sentence and look for a meaning cue.
    - Circle the meaning cue.
    - Double underline the words that define **retire**.
    - Draw an arrow from the word **retire** to the definition.

---

from "Tony Hawk: Extreme Athlete"

Tony retired from professional skateboarding when he was 31. But in skateboarding, the word "retire" doesn't mean he stopped skating. It just means he's stopped competitive skating. He still skates almost every day. He learns new tricks. He does several public demonstrations a year.

---

3. Define the term **retire** in your own words.

_____

_____

4. Verify your definition of the term **retire** by using a dictionary reference source.

Exercise 7 · Answer It

▶ Underline the signal word and answer each question.

▶ Make sure your answer addresses the question.

1. Describe Tony Hawk as an athlete. Use examples from the selection.

_____

_____

_____

_____

2. What can you infer about the goals Tony set for himself as a child?

_____

_____

_____

_____

3. Read this quote from the selection: "Tony started playing on the bright blue board. Crash! Bang! Slam!" The words **crash**, **bang**, and **slam** are examples of onomatopoeia. Explain the effect this type of word has on the reader.

_____

_____

_____

_____

(continued)

Exercise 7 (continued) • **Answer It**

4. Select two of Hawk's accomplishments that you think are the most amazing. Explain why.

_____

_____

_____

_____

_____

_____

5. The sport of skateboarding and Tony Hawk's career declined but later became successful again. The author describes Hawk's rising success with the statement "And the Hawk became the 'Phoenix.'" Explain what the author meant by this statement.

_____

_____

_____

_____

_____

_____

Exercise 1 · Syllable Awareness: Segmentation

▶ Listen to the word your teacher says.

▶ Count the syllables in each word. Write the number in the first column.

▶ Write the letter for each vowel sound you hear in the word.

▶ Mark each vowel with the correct diacritical mark.

- Short vowel sound with a breve (˘).

- Long vowel sound with a macron (ˉ).

- **r**-controlled vowel sound, the vowel before the **r** with a circumflex (ˆ).

	How many syllables do you hear?	First vowel sound	Second vowel sound	Third vowel sound
1.				
2.				
3.				
4.				
5.				
6.				
7.				
8.				
9.				
10.				

Unit 16 · Lesson 4

Exercise 2 · Define It: Prefixed Words

▸ Record the meaning of the prefix **sub-**.

▸ Use the definition of **sub-** to fill in the blanks.

▸ Verify your definition with a dictionary.

1. The prefix **sub-** means _____.

2. **Subsoil** means the soil that is _____.

3. A **subnormal** temperature is one that is _____.

4. **Way** is an old word for **road**. A **subway** travels _____.

5. One meaning of **marine** is *sea or ocean*.

   A **submarine** travels _____.

Exercise 3 · Identify It: Suffixes -ed and -en

▸ Each sentence contains one word ending in **-ed** or **-en**.

▸ In some of these words **-ed** and **-en** are suffixes.

▸ In some of the words the letters **ed** and **en** are not suffixes; they are just part of the word.

▸ Underline each word that ends with **-ed** or **-en**.

▸ Do the examples with your teacher. Then check the appropriate column for the word.

Sentence	Verb Suffix	Adjective Suffix	Not a suffix
Example: Nina's classmates <u>picked</u> up all the trash in the park after the rally.	X		
Example: The <u>perplexed</u> students went in and out of the empty school.		X	
Example: The <u>firemen</u> rush to the fire and put out the flames.			X
1. Clint tossed the antifreeze container into Chan's trunk.			
2. The teacher had over a hundred reports on his desk.			
3. The confused student got on the wrong bus after the class trip.			
4. Carlos composed music for a film about skating.			
5. My amused classmates chose the best act.			

Unit 16 · Lesson 4

Exercise 4 · Rewrite It: Past forms of Irregular Verbs

▸ Read each sentence.

▸ Underline each verb in the sentence.

▸ Rewrite the sentence, changing each verb to the past tense.

▸ Check the chart showing the past tense forms of irregular verbs in the *Student Text*.

1. The extreme athletes overcome difficulties of many types.

_____

_____

2. One boy overtakes the leader and wins the competition.

_____

_____

3. Another becomes a superstar overnight.

_____

_____

4. The organizers of the event sell tickets and make money.

_____

_____

5. A fan mistakes one brother for another.

_____

_____

Exercise 5 · Find It: Past forms of Irregular Verbs

▸ Read the text based on "**Tony Hawk: Extreme Athlete**" with your teacher.

▸ Find all the past forms of irregular verbs and underline them.

Note: There are ten past forms of irregular verbs.

---

based on "Tony Hawk: Extreme Athlete"

Tony Hawk's book about himself was a best seller. He thought about kids with no place to skateboard. He began the Tony Hawk Foundation. It brought skate parks to low-income neighborhoods. In that way Tony gave back to his sport. Skateboarders were very happy. They took risks and became better. They held informal competitions and won the admiration of pals.

Unit 16 · Lesson 4

Exercise 6 · Writing Business Letters

▸ Write a business letter based on the following prompt.

Imagine your town has decided to host an extreme sports competition. Write a business letter to the town's athletic coordinator, Martha Washington, to apply to be a volunteer at the event. The contact information of the athletic coordinator is: 500 Main St., Writersville, VA 11111.

- Underline the purpose of the letter.
- Circle the name of the person who will receive the letter.
- Underline twice the address where you will send the letter.

▸ Write the letter on the lines that are provided. Refer to the Handbook for the format of the letter, as needed.

_____

_____

_____

_____

_____

_____

_____

_____

_____

_____

_____

_____

_____

_____

_____

_____

_____

_____

_____

_____

Exercise 1 · Word Relationships: Antonyms, Synonyms, and Attributes

▶ Read each word pair.

▶ Sort the word pairs according to their relationship.

▶ Discuss your answers with a partner.

admire : respect	arrive : depart	hurricane : wind	secure : safe
parade : drum	provide : give	complete : begin	polite : rude
math : divide	include : exclude	create : make	band : trombone

Antonyms (opposite)	Synonyms (same)	Attributes

Unit 16 · Lesson 5

Exercise 2 · Writing Business Letters

▶ Write a business letter based on the following prompt.

Your town has decided to host an extreme sports competition. You would like to buy tickets. Write a business letter to the head of the recreation department for the town to find out how you can get a schedule and tickets for the events. The contact information for the recreation department is: Writersville Recreation Department, 14 Water St., Writersville, VA 11111

- Underline the purpose of the letter.
- Circle the name of the person who will receive the letter.
- Underline twice the address where you will send the letter.

▶ Word process the letter or write it on a separate piece of paper. Refer to the Handbook for the format of the letter, as needed.

_____

_____

_____

_____

_____

_____

_____

_____

_____

_____

_____

_____

_____

_____

_____

_____

_____

_____

Exercise 1 · Listening for Stressed Syllables

▶ Listen to each word your teacher says. Repeat the word.

▶ Listen for the stressed syllable.

▶ Put an X in the box to mark the position of the stressed syllable.

▶ Listen for schwa in the unstressed syllable. Highlight or circle the vowel when it is reduced to schwa.

Word	1st Syllable	2nd Syllable
1. comprise		
2. invoke		
3. transcribe		
4. purchase		
5. escape		

Unit 16 · Lesson 6

Exercise 2 · Spelling Pretest 2

▸ Listen to the word your teacher repeats.

▸ Write the word.

1. _____   6. _____   11. _____

2. _____   7. _____   12. _____

3. _____   8. _____   13. _____

4. _____   9. _____   14. _____

5. _____   10. _____   15. _____

Exercise 3 · Word Relationships: Analogies

▶ Read the first word pair in each item.

▶ Underline the word that names the relationship: **synonym**, **antonym**, or **attribute**.

▶ Choose a word from the **Word Bank** that has the same relationship to the word in the second part of the analogy.

▶ Write the word in the blank to complete the analogy.

▶ Discuss your answers with a partner.

Word Bank

wind	safe	make
begin	divide	exclude

1. provide : give :: create : _____   Relationship: synonym antonym attribute

2. polite : rude :: complete : _____   Relationship: synonym antonym attribute

3. admire : respect :: secure : _____   Relationship: synonym antonym attribute

4. arrive : depart :: include : _____   Relationship: synonym antonym attribute

5. storm : thunder :: hurricane : _____   Relationship: synonym antonym attribute

Unit 16 · Lesson 6

Exercise 4 · Find It: Adjectives of the Same Kind

▶ Read each sentence.

▶ Find two adjectives of the same kind that modify the same noun.

▶ Underline each of the adjectives.

▶ Circle the conjunction that joins the adjectives.

▶ Draw arrows from both adjectives to the noun they describe.

▶ Do the first sentence with your teacher.

1. Worldwide and international events are held for Special Olympics athletes.

2. Challenging or exciting events sell out quickly.

3. Committed and dedicated athletes attend the Special Olympics.

4. The team could wear red or black sneakers.

5. When athletes finish a race, they feel happy and satisfied.

6. Extreme sports involve risky and daring tricks.

7. Strong but light helmets protect skaters' heads.

8. Slick or uneven pavement can sometimes cause problems.

9. Skaters have developed a new and interesting jargon.

10. The new and colorful expressions are hard for others to understand.

Exercise 5 · Phrase It

▸ Use the penciling strategy to "scoop" the phrases in each sentence.

▸ Read the sentence as you would speak it.

▸ The first two are done for you .

1. Extreme athletes love risks.

2. Extreme skaters are fine athletes.

3. In-line skates are not like skates of the past.

4. They are light, fast, and strong.

5. Skaters use their own jargon.

6. Bashing means going down steps.

7. They take their skating to the next level!

8. Extreme sports have added risks.

9. Without protection, skaters get hurt.

10. Safe athletes wear helmets and use pads.

Unit 16 · Lesson 6

Exercise 6 · Use the Clues: Vocabulary Strategies

▸ Read the sentence pairs.

▸ Read the pronoun that is circled.

▸ Identify the noun that the pronoun replaces in each sentence.

▸ Underline the noun replaced by the pronoun.

▸ Draw an arrow to show the link between the pronoun and the noun it replaces.

1. Extreme athletes love risks. (They) do their sport and add a twist.

2. Extreme skaters use in-line skates. (They)'re not like the skates of the past.

3. Extreme skaters use in-line skates. (They) don't use skating rinks.

4. Take the top of the ramp. (It) has a name.

5. Safe athletes protect themselves. (They) use helmets and pads.

Exercise 7 · Rewrite It: Pronouns

▸ Reread each pair of sentences in Exercise 6, **Use the Clues: Vocabulary Strategies**.

▸ Replace the circled pronoun with the noun or noun phrase that it represents.

▸ Rewrite the sentence using the noun.

▸ Check for sentence signals—capital letters and end punctuation.

▸ Read the new sentence.

▸ Do the first one with your teacher.

1. _____

2. _____

3. _____

4. _____

5. _____

Exercise 1 · Listening for Word Parts

▶ Listen to each word your teacher says.

▶ Mark **Yes** if you hear a suffix or **No** if you don't hear a suffix.

▶ If you hear a suffix, write the suffix you hear.

	Do you hear a suffix on the word?		If **Yes**, what is the suffix?
	Yes	No	
1.			
2.			
3.			
4.			
5.			
6.			
7.			
8.			
9.			
10.			

Exercise 2 · Listening for Stressed Syllables

▸ Listen to each word your teacher says. Repeat the word.

▸ Listen for the stressed syllable.

▸ Make an X in the box to mark the position of the stressed syllable.

▸ Listen for schwa in the unstressed syllable. Highlight or circle the vowel if it is reduced to schwa.

Word	1st Syllable	2nd Syllable	3rd Syllable
1. positive			
2. arrive			
3. exclude			
4. oppose			
5. tribute			

Unit 16 · Lesson 7

Exercise 3 · Divide It

▸ Read each sentence silently.

▸ Use the steps of **Divide It** to break each **boldfaced** word into syllables.

▸ Blend the syllables together to read each boldfaced word.

▸ After decoding all the boldfaced words, read the sentence to a partner.

▸ Follow along with your teacher's example to complete the first item.

1. He was **determined** to **accomplish athletic** feats.

   determined   accomplish   athletic

2. Tony has a six-**figure contract**.

   figure   contract

3. **Extreme** skaters **refine** their skills.

   extreme   refine

4. Skaters use **helmets** so that they don't get **injured**.

   helmets   injured

Exercise 4 · Find It: Contractions

▸ Read the sentences.

▸ Circle the contractions.

▸ Expand each contraction into two words on the lines below.

1. They'd trained Lara for their events.

2. She's been coaching the runners.

3. You'd tried your hardest.

4. It's been a huge accomplishment.

5. He's shown that he is brave.

1. _____

2. _____

3. _____

4. _____

5. _____

Exercise 5 · Find It: Past and Present Participles as Adjectives

▸ Each sentence contains a present or past participle that is used as an adjective.

▸ Underline each participle and copy it into the appropriate column.

▸ Other words in the sentences may end with the letters **-ing**, **-ed**, or **-en**. If they are not participles, do not include them.

▸ Work through the examples with your teacher.

Sentence	Present Participle	Past Participle
Examples: It is hard to kick a deflated football.		
The skidding car crashed into the telephone pole.		
Broken glass littered the sidewalk.		
1. After their walk, the dehydrated hikers sipped water and rested.		
2. Prepared for his final exam, Ted arrived at school that morning with a positive attitude.		
3. The defending champ won the gold medal at the Olympic Games.		
4. The ice on the frozen pond was thick enough for skating.		
5. He read about the exploding flashcube trick in a novel.		
6. The broken posts could not support the huge pile of wood.		
7. The converted sedan became a great race car.		
8. The raging winds tore trees out of the ground.		
9. Bothered by injury, the athlete did not compete.		
10. The developing news story preempted the local news.		

Exercise 6 · Find It: Participial Phrases with Past Participles

▸ Read each sentence.

▸ Look at the underlined noun.

▸ Copy the adjective and participial phrase that describe that noun.

▸ Work through the first two examples with your teacher.

Sentence	*What kind?* or *Which one?*
Example: The athletic <u>girls</u>, dressed in team uniforms, took part in the track meet.	What kind of girls? a. _____ b. _____
Example: The angry <u>chicken</u>, covered in mud, clucked loudly.	What kind of chicken? a. _____ b. _____
1. The loud <u>band</u>, hired by Brad, played all night for his party.	Which band? a. _____ b. _____
2. The brave <u>divers</u>, protected by antishark cages, explored the sea floor.	Which divers? a. _____ b. _____
3. Prepared for the test, the successful <u>student</u> passed with high marks.	Which student? a. _____ b. _____

(continued)

Exercise 6 (continued) · Find It: Participial Phrases with Past Participles

Sentence	What kind? or Which one?
4. The old <u>soldier</u>, decorated with medals, stood at attention.	Which soldier? a. _____ b. _____
5. The unhappy dog, enclosed in the yard, barked all night.	Which dog? a. _____ b. _____

Exercise 7 · Diagram It: Adjectives of the Same Kind

▸ Read each sentence.

▸ Do the first diagram with your teacher.

▸ Make an **X** above the vertical line that separates the complete subject from the complete predicate.

▸ Diagram the remaining sentences on your own.

▸ Review your diagrams and make necessary corrections.

1. Tired but proud runners accepted their medals.

2. Extreme skaters do risky and daring tricks.

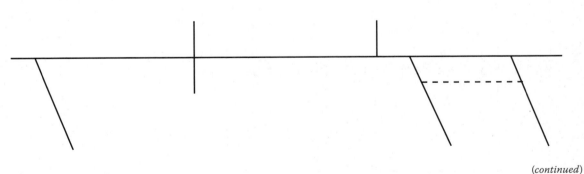

(continued)

Exercise 7 (continued) · Diagram It: Adjectives of the Same Kind

3. Young and old daredevils try extreme sports.

4. Extreme sports capture the vivid and active imaginations of young people.

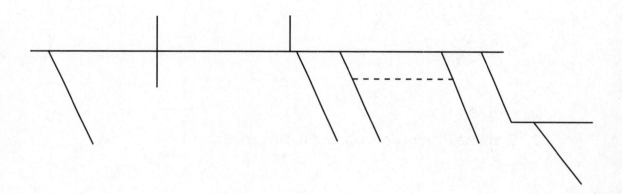

5. Skateboarders live risky but exciting lives.

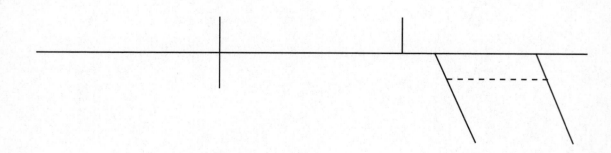

Exercise 8 · Organizing Information: Informal Outline

▶ Read the following prompt:

Write an essay describing how extreme sports can be both fun and dangerous.

▶ Fill out the informal outline. Begin by choosing star ideas for the left side of the outline, and then choose E's (examples, elaboration, and evidence) for the right side of the outline.

★ _____   – _____

                                 • _____

                                   • _____

                           – _____

                                   • _____

                                   • _____

★ _____   – _____

                                   • _____

                                   • _____

                           – _____

                                   • _____

                                   • _____

▶ Use the outline to draft a **Two-Sentence Introductory Paragraph**.

_____

_____

_____

_____

Exercise 1 · Listening for Word Parts

▸ Listen to each word your teacher says.

▸ Mark **Yes** or **No** to show whether the word has a suffix.

▸ If **Yes**, write the suffix.

	Do you hear a suffix on the word?		If **Yes**, what is the suffix?
	Yes	No	
1.			
2.			
3.			
4.			
5.			
6.			
7.			
8.			
9.			
10.			

Exercise 2 · Use the Clues: Vocabulary Strategies

1. Use substitutions along with your teacher to define **unique**.

> Special Olympics are unique, or different, sporting events.

2. Use meaning cues to define **divisions**.
- Underline the vocabulary word **divisions**.
- Read aloud the text before and after and look for a word or words that signal a substitution.
- Circle the word or words that signal the substitution.
- Double underline the word or words you will substitute for **divisions**.
- Draw an arrow from the word **divisions** to its substitution.

---

based on "A Special Kind of Athlete"

Special Olympics is organized with fairness in mind. People of about the same age and ability compete in divisions. Team sports have three age divisions, or groups. This helps participants with more than physical development. It helps their self-esteem. It boosts self-confidence. Everyone has a chance to win.

---

3. Define the term **divisions** in your own words.

_____

_____

_____

4. Verify your definition of the term **divisions** by using a dictionary reference source.

Unit 16 · Lesson 8

Exercise 3 · Answer It: Using Signal Words

‣ Underline the signal word and answer each question.

‣ Check to be sure your answer addresses what the question is asking.

1. Distinguish Special Olympics from the Olympic Games.

_____   _____

_____   _____

_____   _____

_____   _____

_____   _____

_____   _____

_____   _____

_____   _____

2. What can you infer from the Special Olympics Oath about what is important in Special Olympics?

_____

_____

_____

3. Select two events included in Special Olympics that you would like to coach. Tell why you made your selections.

_____

_____

_____

_____

(continued)

Exercise 3 (continued) · Answer It: Using Signal Words

4. Distinguish whether the following statements about Special Olympics are facts or opinions:

   a. Special Olympics began as a day camp. _____

   b. Special Olympics is a great event. _____

   c. Today Special Olympics has 27 official sports. _____

   d. Special Olympics athletes are determined. _____

   e. Special Olympics is different from the Olympic Games. _____

5. What can you infer about Steven Walker's personality?

   _____

   _____

   _____

   _____

Exercise 1 · Listening for Stressed Syllables

▶ Listen to each word your teacher says. Repeat the word.

▶ Listen for the stressed syllable.

▶ Put an X in the box that corresponds to the position of the stressed syllable.

Word	1st Syllable	2nd Syllable	3rd Syllable
1. prescribe			
2. permissive			
3. decline			
4. require			
5. elope			

Exercise 2 · Build It

▸ Create words by combining prefixes and suffixes in the middle square with base words.

Example: sub + divide +ed = subdivided

▸ Record each word you make in the chart on the next page according to the headings.

▸ Use the **Drop e** spelling rule when necessary.

▸ Use a dictionary to verify that you are building real words.

▸ Add any new words that you find.

divide	scribe	mistake
forgive	sub- -ed anti- -en	septic
theft	lock	compact

(continued)

Unit 16 · Lesson 9

Exercise 2 (continued) · Build It

sub-	anti-	other

Exercise 3 · Define It

▸ Record the meaning of the prefix **anti-**.

▸ Use the definition of **anti-** to complete each sentence.

▸ Check your answers in a dictionary.

    1. The prefix **anti-** means _____.

    2. **Antiwar** means _____.

    3. **Septic** means *germs* or *filth*. An **antiseptic** works _____.

    4. The **antihero's** personality is _____ from that of a hero.

    5. **Antifreeze** in a car's radiator protects it _____.

Exercise 4 · Find It: Object of the Preposition

▸ Read the text.

▸ Find and underline each prepositional phrase.

▸ Circle the object of each preposition.

based on "The Complete Athlete"

Shriver helped people with limited skills. She began a summer day camp for them. The camp was for athletes. She held the camp at her home. Trainers for many events came to the camp. Campers learned from the trainers. Some campers became very good at different sports. The campers competed in many events. Every competitor in an event won a medal.

Exercise 5 · Find It: Adjectives of the Same Kind

▸ Read each sentence.

▸ Underline the adjectives of the same kind and the conjunction that joins them.

▸ Circle the noun they modify.

▸ Do the first one with your teacher.

1. Young and eager athletes compete in extreme sports events.

2. Beginners start with small and simple tricks.

3. Skillful athletes try risky and challenging tricks.

4. In-line skaters use skates with light and sturdy wheels.

5. Passersby watch the moves of these brave and graceful skaters.

Exercise 1 · Listening for Stressed Syllables

▸ Listen to the word your teacher says. Repeat the word.

▸ Count the syllables and write the number of syllables in the first column.

▸ Listen as your teacher says the word again. Identify the stressed syllable.

▸ Write the letters for the stressed syllable in the correct column.

	How many syllables do you hear?	First Syllable	Second Syllable
1.			
2.			
3.			
4.			
5.			

Check off the activities you complete with each lesson. Evaluate your accomplishments at the end of each lesson. Pay attention to teacher evaluations and comments.

	Unit Objectives (Lessons 1-5)	Lesson 1 (Date:_____)	Lesson 2 (Date:_____)
STEP 1	• Segment syllables in multisyllable words. • Say the vowel sounds represented by **y** /ĭ/, /ī/, /ē/. • Identify the stress pattern and conditions for each vowel sound represented by **y**.	❑ Review: Consonants and Vowels ❑ Introduce: The Letter **y** ❑ Exercise 1: Listening for Sounds in Words	❑ Phoneme Segmentation ❑ Review: Conditions for Sounds for **y** in Syllables ❑ Multiple Ways to Spell Vowel Sounds ❑ Listening for Sounds in Words
STEP 2	• Read fluently and spell words with sound spelling correspondences, syllable types, and prefixes for this and previous units. • Read fluently and spell the **Essential Words**: *answer, certain, engine, laugh, oil, poor*. • Spell words following the Change **y** rule..	❑ Exercise 2: Spelling Pretest 1 ❑ Memorize It ❑ Handwriting Practice: Timed	❑ Sort It: Sounds for **y** ❑ Introduce: The Change **y** Rule ❑ Change It: The Change **y** Rule ❑ Word Fluency 1 ❑ Memorize It ❑ Handwriting Practice
STEP 3	• Use synonyms, antonyms, word attributes, and relationships to define **Unit Words**. • Use suffixes **-er**, **-est**, and **-ly** to change the meaning of words.	❑ K-W-L Organizer ❑ Expression of the Day	❑ Review: Degrees of Adjectives ❑ Exercise 2: Rewrite It: Comparative and Superlative Adjectives ❑ Expression of the Day
STEP 4	• Write phrases using a possessive noun. • Identify and use adverbs and prepositional phrases that act as adverbs. • Identify **do** as a main verb or helping verb.	❑ Review: Possessive Nouns ❑ Exercise 3: Rewrite It: Possessive Nouns ❑ Review: Possessives ❑ Exercise 4: Identify It: Pronouns ❑ Introduce: Appositives ❑ Exercise 5: Identify It: Appositives	❑ Review: Adverbs ❑ Exercise 3: Find It: Adverbs
STEP 5	• Read phrases and passages fluently. • Preview nonfciton reading selection using text features. • Define vocabulary using context-based strategies. • Read and understand informational text. • Answer multiple-choice comprehension questions.	❑ Exercise 6: Phrase It ❑ Independent Text: **"The Pyramids"**	❑ Passage Fluency 1 ❑ Exercise 4: Use the Clues: Vocabulary Strategies
STEP 6	• Generate sentences using a six-stage process. • Distinguish fact and opinion statements. • Answer comprehension questions using **list**, **organize**, **select**, **explain**, **describe**, **infer**, **tell**, **outline**, and **distinguish**. • Write an expository (explanatory) essay including a two-sentence introductory paragraph, body paragraphs, and a concluding paragraph.	❑ Masterpiece Sentences: Stages 1-3 ❑ Types of Statements: Fact or Opinion?	❑ Essay Structure
	Self-Evaluation (5 is the highest) **Effort** = I produced my best work. **Participation** = I was actively involved in tasks. **Independence** = I worked on my own.	**Effort:** 1 2 3 4 5 **Participation:** 1 2 3 4 5 **Independence:** 1 2 3 4 5	**Effort:** 1 2 3 4 5 **Participation:** 1 2 3 4 5 **Independence:** 1 2 3 4 5
	Teacher Evaluation	**Effort:** 1 2 3 4 5 **Participation:** 1 2 3 4 5 **Independence:** 1 2 3 4 5	**Effort:** 1 2 3 4 5 **Participation:** 1 2 3 4 5 **Independence:** 1 2 3 4 5

Lesson 3 (Date:_____)	Lesson 4 (Date:_____)	Lesson 5 (Date:_____)
❑ Phoneme Segmentation ❑ Phoneme Substitution ❑ Syllable Awareness: Segmentation ❑ Exercise 1: Listening for Sounds in Words	❑ Exercise 1: Syllable Awareness: Segmentation	❑ Content Mastery: Syllable Awareness
❑ Exercise 2: Sort It: Syllable Types ❑ Exercise 3: Find It: Essential Words ❑ Word Fluency 1	❑ Review: The Change **y** Rule ❑ Change It: The Change **y** Rule ❑ Word Fluency 2 ❑ Type It: Essential Words	❑ Content Mastery: Spelling Posttest 1
❑ Exercise 4: Define It ❑ Draw It: Idioms ❑ Expression of the Day	❑ Introduce: Adverb Suffix **-ly** ❑ Exercise 2: Find It: Adverbs ❑ Exercise 3: Rewrite It: Adverbs ❑ Expression of the Day	❑ Review: Word Relationships: Antonyms, Synonyms, and Attributes ❑ Review: Analogies ❑ Exercise 1: Word Relationships: Analogies ❑ Draw It: Idioms ❑ Expression of the Day
❑ Introduce: The Verb **Do** ❑ Exercise 5: Identify It: Main Verb or Helping Verb	❑ Review: Irregular Verbs ❑ Exercise 4: Find It: Past Tense Forms of Irregular Verbs ❑ Tense Timeline ❑ Exercise 5: Rewrite It: Verb Tense	❑ Review: Appositives ❑ Exercise 2: Find It: Appositives ❑ Masterpiece Sentences: Stage 2: Paint Your Predicate
❑ Instructional Text: **"Building a Pyramid"** Exercise 6: Use the Clues	❑ Exercise 6: Understanding Multiple-Choice Comprehension Questions	❑ Review Content and Ideas for an Expository Essay
❑ Exercise 7: Answer It: Using Signal Words	❑ Prepare to Write: Expository (Explanatory) Essay	❑ Write It: Expository Essay
Effort: 1 2 3 4 5 **Participation:** 1 2 3 4 5 **Independence:** 1 2 3 4 5	**Effort:** 1 2 3 4 5 **Participation:** 1 2 3 4 5 **Independence:** 1 2 3 4 5	**Effort:** 1 2 3 4 5 **Participation:** 1 2 3 4 5 **Independence:** 1 2 3 4 5
Effort: 1 2 3 4 5 **Participation:** 1 2 3 4 5 **Independence:** 1 2 3 4 5	**Effort:** 1 2 3 4 5 **Participation:** 1 2 3 4 5 **Independence:** 1 2 3 4 5	**Effort:** 1 2 3 4 5 **Participation:** 1 2 3 4 5 **Independence:** 1 2 3 4 5

Check off the activities you complete with each lesson. Evaluate your accomplishments at the end of each lesson. Pay attention to teacher evaluations and comments.

	Unit Objectives (Lessons 6-10)	Lesson 6 (Date:_____)	Lesson 7 (Date:_____)
STEP 1	• Segment syllables in multisyllable words. • Say the vowel sounds represented by **y** / ĭ /, / ī /, / ē /. • Identify the stress pattern and conditions for each vowel sound represented by **y**.	❑ Review: Schwa ❑ Exercise 1: Listening for Stressed Syllables	❑ Exercise 1: Listening for Stressed Syllables ❑ Exercise 2: Listening for Word Parts
STEP 2	• Read fluently and spell words with sound spelling correspondences, syllable types, and prefixes for this and previous units. • Read fluently and spell the **Essential Words**: *answer, certain, engine, laugh, oil, poor.*	❑ Exercise 2: Spelling Pretest 2 ❑ Word Fluency 3 ❑ Handwriting Practice: Timed	❑ Word Fluency 4 ❑ Exercise 3: Build It: Prefixed Words
STEP 3	• Use synonyms, antonyms, word attributes, and relationships to define **Unit Words**. • Use suffixes **-er**, **-est**, and **-ly** to change the meaning of words.	❑ K-W-L Organizer ❑ Expression of the Day	❑ Exercise 4: Define It: Prefixes **con-** and **trans-** ❑ Expression of the Day
STEP 4	• Write phrases using a possessive noun. • Identify and use adverbs and prepositional phrases that act as adverbs. • Identify **do** as a main verb or helping verb. • Identify and analyze sentences with indirect objects.	❑ Introduce: Indirect Objects ❑ Exercise 3: Identify It: Direct and Indirect Objects ❑ Exercise 4: Find It: Direct and Indirect Objects	❑ Review: Indirect Objects ❑ Exercise 5: Find It: Indirect Objects ❑ Exercise 6: Rewrite It: Indirect Objects
STEP 5	• Read phrases and passages fluently. • Preview nonfcition reading selection using text features. • Define vocabulary using context-based strategies. • Read and understand informational text. • Answer multiple-choice comprehension questions.	❑ Exercise 5: Phrase It ❑ Independent Text: **"Living in Europe"** Exercise 6: Use the Clues	❑ Passage Fluency 2
STEP 6	• Answer comprehension questions using **list, organize, select, explain, describe, infer, tell, outline,** and **distinguish**. • Write an expository (explanatory) essay including a two-sentence introductory paragraph, body paragraphs, and a concluding paragraph. • Edit and revise an expository (explanatory) essay.	❑ Exercise 7: Rewrite It	❑ Essay Structure
	Self-Evaluation (5 is the highest) **Effort** = I produced my best work. **Participation** = I was actively involved in tasks. **Independence** = I worked on my own.	**Effort:** 1 2 3 4 5 **Participation:** 1 2 3 4 5 **Independence:** 1 2 3 4 5	**Effort:** 1 2 3 4 5 **Participation:** 1 2 3 4 5 **Independence:** 1 2 3 4 5
	Teacher Evaluation	**Effort:** 1 2 3 4 5 **Participation:** 1 2 3 4 5 **Independence:** 1 2 3 4 5	**Effort:** 1 2 3 4 5 **Participation:** 1 2 3 4 5 **Independence:** 1 2 3 4 5

Lesson 8 (Date:_____)	Lesson 9 (Date:_____)	Lesson 10 (Date:_____)
❑ Exercise 1: Listening for Word Parts	❑ Exercise 1: Listening for Stressed Syllables	❑ Exercise 1: Listening for Stressed Syllables
❑ Review: Divide It ❑ Exercise 2: Divide It	❑ Exercise 2: Build It	❑ Content Mastery: Spelling Posttest 2
❑ Content Mastery: Word Relationships; Suffixes	❑ Introduce: Forms of the Prefix **con-** ❑ Exercise 3: Define It: Forms of the Prefix **con-** ❑ Exercise 4: Fill-in: Forms of the Prefix **con-** ❑ Expression of the Day	❑ Exercise 2: Sort It: Meaning Categories ❑ Expression of the Day
❑ Exercise 3: Diagram It: Indirect Objects	❑ Exercise 5: Find It: Indirect Objects ❑ Review: **Have** in Perfect Tense Verbs ❑ Exercise 6: Identify It: **Have** in Perfect Tense Verbs	❑ Content Mastery: Possessive Nouns; Adverbs; **Do**—Main Verb or Helping Verb; and Indirect Objects
❑ Instructional Text: **"Growing Up Egyptian"** Exercise 4: Use the Clues	❑ Exercise 7: Answering Multiple-Choice and Open-Ended Comprehension Questions	❑ Oral Presentation of Expository Essays
❑ Exercise 5: Answer It: Using Signal Words	❑ Write It: Expository Essay	❑ Check It: Review Writer's Checklist ❑ Revise It: Expository Essay
Effort: 1 2 3 4 5 **Participation:** 1 2 3 4 5 **Independence:** 1 2 3 4 5	**Effort:** 1 2 3 4 5 **Participation:** 1 2 3 4 5 **Independence:** 1 2 3 4 5	**Effort:** 1 2 3 4 5 **Participation:** 1 2 3 4 5 **Independence:** 1 2 3 4 5
Effort: 1 2 3 4 5 **Participation:** 1 2 3 4 5 **Independence:** 1 2 3 4 5	**Effort:** 1 2 3 4 5 **Participation:** 1 2 3 4 5 **Independence:** 1 2 3 4 5	**Effort:** 1 2 3 4 5 **Participation:** 1 2 3 4 5 **Independence:** 1 2 3 4 5

Exercise 1 · Listening for Sounds in Words

▸ Listen to each word your teacher says.

▸ Put an X in the column to show what vowel sound you hear in the syllable that your teacher indicates.

	Long **i**	Long **e**	Short **i**
1.			
2.			
3.			
4.			
5.			
6.			
7.			
8.			
9.			
10.			

Exercise 2 · Spelling Pretest 1

▸ Write the word your teacher repeats.

1. _____
2. _____
3. _____
4. _____
5. _____

6. _____
7. _____
8. _____
9. _____
10. _____

11. _____
12. _____
13. _____
14. _____
15. _____

Exercise 3 · Rewrite It: Possessive Nouns

▸ Read each sentence.

▸ Change the underlined words in each sentence to a phrase with a possessive noun.

▸ Write the phrase on the line.

▸ Do the first sentence along with your teacher.

1. <u>The base of the pyramid</u> had four corners. _____

2. Workers chipped and carved <u>the shape of each stone</u>. _____

3. <u>The waters of the Nile</u> were used to move the stone. _____

4. <u>The tools of the workers</u> were chisels and stone hammers. _____

5. Pyramids were used for <u>the graves of kings</u>. _____

6. <u>The weight of one block</u> could be seventy tons. _____

7. <u>The methods of the workers</u> involved many steps. _____

8. <u>The day of the worker</u> was long and hard. _____

9. Today we can see <u>the glory of the pyramids</u>. _____

10. We marvel at <u>the construction of the pyramid</u>. _____

Unit 17 · Lesson 1

Exercise 4 · Identify It: Pronouns

▸ Read each sentence and decide if the underlined pronoun is a subject, object, or possessive pronoun.

▸ Copy the pronoun into the correct column on the chart.

1. People of Egypt are proud the pyramids are <u>theirs</u>.

2. <u>They</u> offer trips by camel to see them.

3. That book with photos of Egypt is <u>mine</u>.

4. The men showed the blocks the stonecutters made to <u>us</u>.

5. Their way of building was different from <u>ours</u>.

6. A stonecutter sharpened the tools that were <u>his</u>.

7. He kept <u>them</u> in a safe place.

8. <u>He</u> would give his son his tools.

9. A father would offer his son help to use <u>them</u>.

10. <u>You</u> should visit the pyramids too.

	Nominative	Object	Possessive
1.			
2.			
3.			
4.			
5.			
6.			
7.			
8.			
9.			
10.			

Exercise 5 · Identify It: Appositives

▸ Read each sentence and underline the appositive and any words that modify it.

▸ Place commas as needed.

▸ Do the first sentence with your teacher.

1. Moses helps his father a farmer.

2. The farm is near a great river the Nile.

3. The farms main crop wheat is ripe.

4. Moses a hard worker cuts the wheat.

5. The wheat will be made into bread a staple food.

Unit 17 · Lesson 1

Exercise 6 · Phrase It

▸ Use a pencil to "scoop" the phrases in each sentence.

▸ Read each sentence as you would speak it.

▸ The first two sentences are done for you as examples.

1. The pyramids were constructed long ago.

2. It seems like an impossible task.

3. They made huge numbers of blocks.

4. One base block was big.

5. Their method involved steps.

6. First, they dug the stone.

7. Then, it was put on a raft.

8. The raft drifted down the Nile River.

9. At the site, the stone was taken off.

10. Workers carved a channel into the stone.

Exercise 1 · Sort It: Vowel Sounds for y

▸ Read the words in the **Word Bank**.

▸ Sort each word according to the vowel sound represented by the letter **y** by writing the word under the correct heading.

Word Bank

type	army	copy	byte
dry	happy	party	hype
rye	by	story	tiny

long i	long e

Exercise 2 · Rewrite It: Comparative and Superlative Adjectives

▸ Read the adjectives.

▸ Add **-er** or the word **more** to make the comparative form of each adjective.

▸ Add **-est** or the word **most** to make the superlative form of the adjective.

▸ Use the **Change y Rule** when necessary.

Adjective	Comparative	Superlative
1. dark	_____	_____
2. western	_____	_____
3. carsick	_____	_____
4. silly	_____	_____
5. happy	_____	_____

What job does the word with the **-er** suffix have?

_____

What job does the word with the **-est** suffix have?

_____

When do we use **more** and **most** with the adjective?

_____

_____

Write two sentences using comparative and superlative adjectives from the task above.

_____

_____

_____

_____

Exercise 3 · Find It: Adverbs

▸ Read each sentence.

▸ Find and underline the adverb or prepositional phrase that acts like an adverb in each sentence.

▸ Decide if the word or phrase tells **how**, **when**, or **where**.

▸ Mark the correct column to show your choice.

	how	when	where
1. The Egyptian pyramids were built in the desert.			
2. Huge stone blocks were piled atop each other.			
3. The workers hammered the stones forcefully.			
4. All year long, the work continued.			
5. Expert workers shaped the stones precisely.			
6. They used hand tools then.			
7. Workers sculpted the stones into shapes.			
8. One huge stone fell through the base.			
9. The stone split with a loud crack.			
10. Stone fragments gashed workers on their arms.			

Exercise 4 · Use the Clues: Vocabulary Strategies

▶ Read each pair of sentences.

▶ Find the pronoun that is circled.

▶ Identify the noun that the pronoun replaces and underline it.

▶ Draw an arrow to show the link between the pronoun and the noun it replaces.

▶ Do the first sentence along with your teacher.

1. (It) was made long ago. It's a pyramid!

2. Why were pyramids constructed? First, (they) were sacred sites.

3. They drenched the wedge in water. (It) expanded.

4. At last, the stone split. They cut (it).

5. (It) was finished. Another amazing pyramid!

Exercise 1 · Listening for Sounds in Words

▸ Listen to each word your teacher says.

▸ Put an X in the column to indicate which long vowel sound you hear.

	/ ē /	/ ī /
1.		
2.		
3.		
4.		
5.		
6.		
7.		
8.		
9.		
10.		

Unit 17 · Lesson 3

Exercise 2 · Sort It: Syllable Types

▸ Read the syllables in the **Word Bank**.

▸ Sort the syllables according to their syllable type by writing each syllable under the correct heading.

Word Bank

cop	byte	my	y	gym
ar	prop	type	ti	tem
er	rye	ny	ty	sys

closed	final silent _e_	open	r-controlled

Exercise 3 · Find It: Essential Words

▸ Write the **Essential Words** in the spaces.

_____ _____ _____

_____ _____ _____

▸ Find the **Essential Words** for this unit in these sentences.

▸ Underline each. There may be more than one in a sentence.

▸ Use your **Essential Word Cards** if you need help.

1. Type your answer quickly.

2. Make certain that fence is on your property.

3. Why is the oil all over the engine?

4. I had to laugh when the mummy came to the door.

5. The poor baby needed to be held.

Exercise 4 · Define It

▸ Fill in the blanks with a category and an attribute to define the word.

▸ Compare any definition that you're unsure of with a dictionary definition.

▸ Do the first word with your teacher.

1. A **pyramid** is _____ that _____
                           category   **attribute(s)**

   _____.

2. An **army** is _____ who _____
                           category   **attribute(s)**

   _____.

3. An **eye** is _____ that _____

   _____.

4. **Happy** is _____ that _____

   _____.

5. A **lady** is _____ who _____

   _____.

6. A **party** is _____ that _____

   _____.

(continued)

Exercise 4 (continued) · Define It

7. An **engine** is _____ that _____

_____ .

8. A **bunny** is _____ that _____

_____ .

9. A **contract** is _____ that _____

_____ .

10. A **pony** is _____ that _____

_____

Identify the words that you defined which name types of **mammals**.

▶ Write the words in the blanks.

_____   _____   _____

_____   _____

Exercise 5 · Identify It: Main Verb or Helping Verb

▸ Read each sentence.

▸ Underline the verb or verb phrase.

▸ Decide if the form of the verb **do** is used as a main verb or a helping verb.

▸ Fill in the correct bubble to show your choice.

▸ Do the first sentence with your teacher.

	Main Verb	Helping Verb
1. The Egyptians did build the pyramids.	◯	◯
2. In those days, men did all the work by hand.	◯	◯
3. The pyramids do have four sides.	◯	◯
4. Some do their work quickly.	◯	◯
5. All the men do their jobs with commitment.	◯	◯
6. A raft does transport cargo on the Nile.	◯	◯
7. The workers did complete repairs on the sites.	◯	◯
8. One stonecutter does his trade extremely well.	◯	◯
9. They will be doing more repairs in the future.	◯	◯
10. The students did study for their test about the pyramids.	◯	◯

Exercise 6 · Use the Clues: Vocabulary Strategies

1. Work with your teacher to use context cues to define **quarries**.

   Builders wanted the pyramids to be close to the stone quarries from which they extracted blocks that weighed as much as seventy tons.

2. Use context cues to define **leveled**.
   - ▸ Underline the unfamiliar word.
   - ▸ Read the text surrounding the word.
   - ▸ Double underline any context cues you find.

   from "Building a Pyramid"

   Next, the ground and building materials were prepared. The ground had to be leveled before any stones could be placed. To do this, workers may have dug a series of trenches into the land and flooded them with water. The water acted like a level. Workers dug earthen "islands" between the trenches to match the level of the water.

3. Define the term **leveled** in your own words.

   _____

   _____

   _____

4. Verify your definition of the term **leveled** by using a dictionary reference source.

Unit 17 · Lesson 3

Exercise 7 · Answer It: Using Signal Words

▶ Underline each signal word you find and think about what it asks you to do.

▶ Answer each question.

▶ Make sure your answer addresses the question.

1. List three major tasks involved in building a pyramid and organize them in the proper sequence. Use transition words to make the order of the tasks clear.

   _____

   _____

   _____

2. Before building a pyramid, workers used a series of steps to level the ground before any stones were placed. Organize the following steps into the correct sequence.

   a. dug the earth between trenches to match the level of the water

   b. flooded ditches with water

   c. dug a series of trenches

   _____

   _____

   _____

3. Throughout the article, the author states several intriguing, or mysterious, facts about the Egyptian pyramids. Select one intriguing fact. Explain why that fact is intriguing to you.

   _____

   _____

   _____

   _____

   _____

   _____

(continued)

Exercise 7 (continued) · Answer It: Using Signal Words

4. The shape of a pyramid may have had different meanings to the ancient Egyptians. Describe the possible meanings of the pyramid shape mentioned in the article.

_____

_____

_____

_____

_____

_____

_____

5. What can you infer about the people who built the pyramids?

_____

_____

_____

Exercise 1 · Syllable Awareness: Segmentation

▶ Listen to the word your teacher says.

▶ Count the syllables. Write the number in the first column.

▶ Write the letter and diacritical mark to stand for each vowel sound you hear.

- Mark short vowel sounds with a breve (˘).

- Mark long vowel sounds with a macron (ˉ).

- For **r**-controlled vowel sounds, mark the vowel before the **r** with a circumflex (ˆ).

	How many syllables do you hear?	First vowel sound	Second vowel sound	Third vowel sound	Fourth vowel sound
1.					
2.					
3.					
4.					
5.					
6.					
7.					
8.					
9.					
10.					

Exercise 2 · Find It: Adverbs

▸ Each sentence contains an adverb ending in **-ly**.

▸ Underline the adverb ending in **-ly**, and draw an arrow from it to the verb it modifies.
Hint: Adverbs do not have to be next to the verb they modify.

Sentences	Answer the question.
Example: Luis <u>quickly</u> answered the ringing phone.	How did Luis answer? **quickly**
Example: His friend Hakim asked him <u>politely</u> if he wanted to watch a video with his family.	How did Hakim ask? **politely**
Example: Now his father had <u>gladly</u> rented another old film.	How did his father rent? **gladly**
1. The boys had recently studied about mummies from ancient Egypt in school.	When did the boys study?
2. Happily, they found an old horror movie about a mummy.	How did they find the movie?
3. The action of the film began calmly enough in Egypt in 1921.	In what way did the action begin?
4. After digging for several months, an archeologist, Sir Joseph Wemple, finally discovered a mummy in a crypt.	When did Wemple discover the mummy?
5. The ancient Egyptians preserved this mummy's body perfectly.	How did they preserve the body?

Unit 17 · Lesson 4

Exercise 3 · Rewrite It: Adverbs

▸ Underline the prepositional phrase that begins with **in** and ends in **way**.

▸ Change the adjective that modifies **way** into an adverb by adding **-ly**.

▸ Read the sentence with the adverb replacing the underlined prepositional phrase.

▸ Write the adverb made from the adjective in the column titled **Adverb**.

Sentence	Adverb
Example: In a quick way, I went back to my homework to read about cats in ancient Egypt.	quickly
1. Ancient Egyptians treated cats in a wonderful way.	
2. They wanted to respect cats for the job they did killing the mice in a rapid way, which protected the stored grain.	
3. In a real way, all cats were property of the Pharaoh.	
4. It was a crime to harm a cat even in a mistaken way.	
5. A person who harmed a cat was punished in a bad way.	

Exercise 4 · Find It: Forms of Irregular Verbs

▸ Read the text below.

▸ Find and underline all the past tense forms of irregular verbs.

▸ Copy the irregular past tense verbs on the lines below.

> The pyramids were constructed long ago. They took a long time to
> build. Men worked hard and time flew. The workers did not have
> wheels or many tools. Sometimes they lent each other their tools.
> If a worker mistook directions, he placed stones incorrectly. When
> the pyramids were complete, they stood in the desert and shone in
> the sun for all to see. The pyramids have withstood the passing of
> time well.

_____   _____   _____

_____   _____   _____

_____   _____   _____

_____

Unit 17 · Lesson 4

Exercise 5 · Rewrite It: Verb Tense

▸ Read each sentence.

▸ Write the verb under the correct position on the **Tense Timeline**.

▸ Expand the verb to include the two additional verb forms on the **Tense Timeline**, following your teacher's example.

Past	Present	Future
Yesterday	Today	Tomorrow

1. Stonecutters **do** their tasks with great skill.

2. Workers **lent** their tools to each other.

3. He **will do** the extra work.

4. Birds **flew** over the pyramids.

5. The worker **will lend** his hammer.

Exercise 6 · Answering Multiple-Choice Comprehension Questions

▸ Read each question and answer choices.

▸ Use **"Building a Pyramid"** from the *Student Text* to help you choose the correct answer.

▸ Fill in the bubble for the correct answer.

1. Which sentence uses the underlined word correctly?
   Ⓐ The woman complained that the new shoes hurt her <u>feat</u>.
   Ⓑ Finishing the test in the time allowed was quite a <u>feat</u>.
   Ⓒ The mountain climbers were proud of their latest <u>feet</u>.
   Ⓓ One of the <u>feat</u> on the table was broken.

2. Pyramids were built near quarries because
   Ⓐ the pharaohs lived there.
   Ⓑ the trucks and trains went by them.
   Ⓒ the builders could not move the rocks long distances.
   Ⓓ the wagons that carried the rocks were kept there.

3. The builders of the pyramids used ramps to
   Ⓐ make the sledges strong.
   Ⓑ move rocks from the quarry and up the pyramid.
   Ⓒ help them mark precise intervals.
   Ⓓ drive wooden wedges into the rocks.

4. The builders of the pyramids most likely leveled the ground because they
   Ⓐ wanted the pyramids to be precise.
   Ⓑ wanted to flood trenches with water.
   Ⓒ needed to dig earth islands.
   Ⓓ needed to split the large rocks.

5. Which of the following sentences from the passage is an opinion about pyramids?
   Ⓐ Traces of these markings remain.
   Ⓑ They are mysterious.
   Ⓒ They flooded these ditches with water.
   Ⓓ Pyramids are tombs.

Exercise 1 · Word Relationships: Analogies

▸ Read the word pair in the first column.

▸ Think about the relationship between the words in the word pair.

▸ Underline **synonym**, **antonym**, or **attribute** to identify the relationship.

▸ Write a word from the **Word Bank** to complete the second word pair so that these words have the relationship you underlined.

▸ Work with a partner to check that both word pairs in the analogy have the same relationship.

Word Bank

rely	pretty	colt	tiny	byte
contrast	big	system	pony	harmony

Analogy	Relationship		
1. rude : polite :: ugly : _____	synonym	antonym	attribute
2. thought : idea :: method :_____	synonym	antonym	attribute
3. poor : rich :: conflict : _____	synonym	antonym	attribute
4. measure : inch :: memory : _____	synonym	antonym	attribute
5. adult : horse :: baby : _____	synonym	antonym	attribute
6. hop : rabbit :: gallop : _____	synonym	antonym	attribute
7. byte : small :: gigabyte : _____	synonym	antonym	attribute
8. huge : big :: small : _____	synonym	antonym	attribute
9. answer : question :: compare : _____	synonym	antonym	attribute
10. imply : infer :: depend : _____	synonym	antonym	attribute

Exercise 2 · Find It: Appositives

▸ Reread each sentence.

▸ Underline the noun that is an appositive.

▸ Circle the appositive and any modifiers.

▸ Draw an arrow from the circle to the noun that the appositive explains, renames, or identifies.

▸ Do the first sentence with your teacher.

1. The museum displayed a mummy, a preserved body.

2. The mummy had been found in a pyramid, a four-sided building with a pointed top.

3. One visitor, a tall lady, stared for a long time.

4. The museum director, Mrs. Hobbs, saw her and introduced herself.

5. The tall lady, a history teacher, asked the director many questions.

Exercise 1 · Listening for Stressed Syllables

▶ Listen to the word your teacher says.

▶ Repeat the word.

▶ Listen for the stressed, or accented, syllable.

▶ Mark an X in the box to mark the position of the stressed, or accented, syllable.

Word	First Syllable	Second Syllable	Third Syllable	Fourth Syllable
1. deny				
2. copy				
3. density				
4. priority				
5. exactly				

Exercise 2 · Spelling Pretest 2

▶ Write the word your teacher repeats.

1. _____   6. _____   11. _____

2. _____   7. _____   12. _____

3. _____   8. _____   13. _____

4. _____   9. _____   14. _____

5. _____   10. _____   15. _____

Exercise 3 · Identify It: Direct and Indirect Objects

▸ Reread each sentence.

▸ Decide if the underlined noun is a direct object or an indirect object.

▸ Put an X in the correct column.

	Indirect Object	Direct Object
1. Helpers bring the <u>workers</u> their lunch.		
2. The father handed Hebeny the scribe's <u>pen</u>.		
3. The boss forgave <u>Moses</u> his mistake.		
4. The king granted the men <u>freedom</u>.		
5. The elders tell young Egyptian <u>boys</u> stories.		

Exercise 4 · Find It: Direct and Indirect Objects

▸ Read each sentence.

▸ Find and underline the indirect object and direct object.

▸ Copy the indirect object and direct object into the correct columns.

	Indirect Object	Direct Object
1. The bosses gave the men a master plan.		
2. The rafts brought the stonecutters large blocks.		
3. The stonecutter lent the worker his tools.		
4. Almost always, a scribe handed his son his job.		
5. Their jobs gave scribes many unusual favors.		

Exercise 5 · Phrase It

▶ Use the penciling strategy to "scoop" the phrases in each sentence.

▶ Read the sentence as you would speak it.

▶ The first two are done for you.

1. In Egypt, people depend on farmers.

2. They supply all the crops.

3. The Nile River floods from June to September.

4. Their lands are covered with water.

5. When the river floods, they work elsewhere.

6. Many farmers work on pyramids.

7. Hebeny's father is a scribe.

8. It is one job that requires a formal education.

9. The writing is done with a code.

10. Hebeny wants to master the skill.

Exercise 6 · Use the Clues: Vocabulary Strategies

▶ Read each sentence pair.

▶ Read the pronoun that is circled.

▶ Identify the noun that the pronoun replaces and underline it.

▶ Draw an arrow to show the link between the pronoun and the noun it replaces.

1. First, meet Moses. (He) is a farmer's son.

2. In Egypt, the public depends on farmers. (They) supply all the crops.

3. Moses helps his dad. He gathers crops. He covers (them) to protect them.

4. Moses helps his dad. He gathers crops. (He) covers them to protect them.

5. Hebeny studies hard. (She) wants to become a scribe.

Unit 17 · Lesson 6

Exercise 7 · Rewrite It

▸ Read the sentences based on **"Living in Egypt."**

▸ Replace each underlined pronoun with a noun and each underlined noun with a pronoun.

▸ Rewrite the sentences.

▸ Read your sentences to the class.

1. At harvest time, <u>Moses</u> helps his dad.

_____

_____

2. When the river floods, <u>they</u> work elsewhere.

_____

_____

3. When the river subsides, <u>they</u> return home.

_____

_____

4. <u>Hebeny</u> studies hard.

_____

_____

5. <u>She</u> wants to be a scribe.

_____

_____

Exercise 1 · Listening for Stressed Syllables

▶ Listen to the word your teacher says. Repeat the word.

▶ Listen for the stressed, or accented, syllable.

▶ Put an X in the box to mark the position of the stressed, or accented, syllable.

Word	First Syllable	Second Syllable	Third Syllable	Fourth Syllable
1. fryer				
2. happy				
3. nobility				
4. enzyme				
5. synopsis				

Unit 17 · Lesson 7

Exercise 2 · Listening for Word Parts

▸ Listen to each word your teacher says.

▸ Mark **Yes** or **No** to show whether the word has a suffix.

▸ If **Yes**, write the suffix.

	Do you hear a suffix on the word?		If **Yes**, what is the suffix?
	Yes	No	
1.			
2.			
3.			
4.			
5.			
6.			
7.			
8.			
9.			
10.			

Exercise 3 · Build It: Prefixed Words

▶ Read the prefixes and syllables in the box.

▶ Combine the syllables with **con-** and **trans-** to make words.

▶ Record the words on the lines.

▶ Check a dictionary to verify that words are real words.

con-	fuse	plant	form
trans-	mit	figure	gress

_____ _____ _____

_____ _____ _____

_____ _____ _____

Unit 17 · Lesson 7

Exercise 4 · Define It: Prefixes con- and trans-

▸ Record the meaning of the prefix **con-**.

▸ Use the definition of the prefix to help define the underlined word in each sentence.

▸ Verify your definition with a dictionary.

1. **Con-** is a prefix meaning _____.

2. The word part **nect** means *join*. When you **connect** something. you

   _____ something else.

3. The word part **fuse** can mean *melt* or *mix up*. **Confuse** means

   _____.

4. The word part **fine** can mean *to border*. **Confine** means _____.

5. The word **text** can mean *words*. **Context** means

   _____.

▸ Record the meaning of the prefix **trans-**.

▸ Use the definition of the prefix to help define the underlined word in each sentence.

▸ Verify your definition with a dictionary.

6. **Trans-** is a prefix meaning _____.

7. A **transatlantic** flight flies _____.

8. The word part **port** means *carry*. When you **transport** goods across the ocean,

   you _____ the ocean.

9. The word part **late** can also mean *to carry or bring*. When you **translate** a word

   from one language to another, you _____

   _____.

10. The word part **fuse** can mean *to pour* or *to move a liquid*. When a doctor

    transfuses blood, she moves it _____.

Exercise 5 · Find It: Indirect Objects

▸ Read each sentence.

▸ Find and underline the indirect object.

1. The scribe's job gave him respect in the community.

2. The worker handed him his tools.

3. Ancient Egyptians rarely gave them the chance to attend school.

4. The girl's mother sold her a fine robe.

5. The stonecutter showed us his work.

Unit 17 · Lesson 7

Exercise 6 · Rewrite It: Indirect Objects

▸ Read each sentence.

▸ Find and underline the indirect object.

▸ Rewrite the sentence, replacing the noun that is the indirect object with a pronoun. Change others words as necessary.

1. The scribe gave his son lessons.

   _____

2. Old tales tell modern people the history of long ago.

   _____

3. The teacher gave Maria and me a book and pencil for our report.

   _____

4. Our report must tell the class the story of the pyramids.

   _____

5. The teacher gave the report a good grade.

   _____

Exercise 1 · Listening for Word Parts

▸ Listen to each word your teacher says.

▸ Mark **Yes** or **No** to tell if you hear a suffix.

▸ If **Yes**, write the suffix.

	Do you hear a suffix on the word?		If **Yes**, what is the suffix?
	Yes	No	
1.			
2.			
3.			
4.			
5.			
6.			
7.			
8.			
9.			
10.			

Exercise 2 · Divide It

▶ Use the steps of **Divide It** to break the words into syllables.

▶ Blend the syllables together to read the word.

1. sloppy

2. ugly

3. levy

4. copy

5. navy

6. lazy

7. forty

8. army

9. ivy

10. imply

Exercise 3 · Diagram It: Indirect Objects

▶ Read each sentence.

▶ Diagram the first sentence with your teacher.

▶ Write an X above the vertical line that separates the complete subject from the complete predicate.

▶ Diagram the remaining sentences independently.

1. The boy's father gave him lessons.

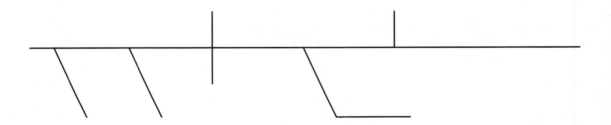

2. Ancient Egyptians did not give girls many chances for education.

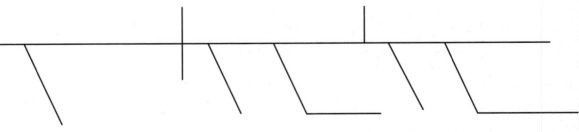

(continued)

Exercise 3 (continued) • Diagram It: Indirect Objects

3. The worker handed him his tools.

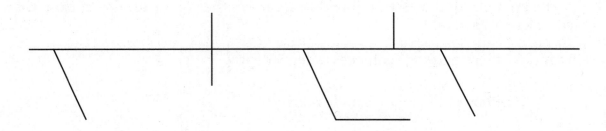

4. The girl's mother sold her a fine robe.

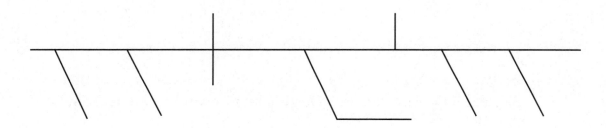

5. The stonecutter showed us his work.

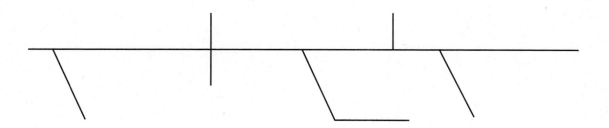

Exercise 4 · Use the Clues: Vocabulary Strategies

1. Work with your teacher to use meaning cues to define **hieroglyphs**.

   Instead of using letters to represent sounds, the ancient Egyptians used hieroglyphs (picture symbols that represent words).

2. Use meaning cues to define **scribe**.
   - ▸ Underline the unfamiliar word.
   - ▸ Look for meaning cues, such as **parentheses ( )**. Circle these.
   - ▸ Double underline the text that defines **scribe**.
   - ▸ Draw an arrow from **scribe** to its definition.

   > **based on "Growing Up Egyptian"**
   >
   > If you were a child in ancient Egypt the size of your home depended on your father's job. Was he the pharaoh? Then your mud-brick home would be a palace with many rooms. Was he a nobleman or a scribe (one of the few people who could write)? If so, your large house may have had a private courtyard with flowers and a fish pond.

3. Define the word **scribe** in your own words:

   _____

   _____

   _____

4. Verify your definition of the term **scribe** by using a dictionary reference source.

Unit 17 · Lesson 8

Exercise 5 · Answer It: Using Signal Words

▸ Underline each signal word you find and think about what it asks you to do.

▸ Answer each question.

▸ Make sure your answer addresses the question.

1. List four things that children in ancient Egypt did which children today still do.

   _____

   _____

   _____

   _____

2. Refer to lines 101–104 in **"Growing Up Egyptian,"** in the *Student Text* and select the type of house that you would like to own if you lived in ancient Egypt. Tell what you would have to do in order to own that type of house.

   _____

   _____

   _____

   _____

3. Tell why it was difficult to learn the ancient Egyptian language.

   _____

   _____

   _____

   _____

(continued)

Exercise 5 (continued) · Answer It: Using Signal Words

4. Reread lines 50–64. Outline the way that students learned to become scribes. Be sure to provide main ideas and supporting details in your outline.

1) _____

   a) _____

   b) _____

   c) _____

2) _____

   a) _____

   b) _____

   c) _____

5. Distinguish between the career choices that teenagers in the United States have today and the career choices that teenagers had in ancient Egypt.

_____

_____

_____

_____

_____

_____

_____

_____

Exercise 1 · Listening for Stressed Syllables

▸ Listen to each word your teacher says. Repeat the word.

▸ Listen for the stressed, or accented, syllable.

▸ Put an X in the box to mark the position of the stressed, or accented, syllable.

Word	First Syllable	Second Syllable	Third Syllable
1. hypnosis			
2. sixty			
3. reply			
4. transact			
5. hurry			

Exercise 2 · Build It

▸ Combine prefixes in the middle square with base words to form words.
Example: com- + mit = commit

▸ Record the words in the chart that follows according to the prefix.

▸ Use a dictionary to verify that you are building real words.

form	verse	late
fer	com- con- col- trans-	mit
pose	gress	spire

(continued)

Exercise 2 (continued) · Build It

col-	com-	con-	trans-

Exercise 3 · Define It: Forms of the Prefix con-

▸ Fill in the blanks to complete the definitions of words using forms of **con-**.

▸ Use a dictionary for extra help if necessary.

1. The prefixes **con-**, **col-**, **cor-**, **co-**, and **com-** can mean

   _____ or _____.

2. **Conjoined** twins are _____ each other or together.

3. When you **cosign** a contract, you _____ someone else.

4. The word part **lide** can mean *hit*.

   When two ships **collide**, they _____ each other.

5. When you **correspond** with someone, you _____ that person by letter or e-mail.

Exercise 4 · Fill-In: Forms of the Prefix con-

▸ Use the prefix **con-** or one of its forms in the **Prefix Box** to complete the word in each sentence.

▸ Read the sentence to make sure you formed the correct word.

▸ Use a dictionary to check the word.

▸ Copy the completed whole word.

Prefix Box

co-	col-	com-	con-	cor-

Sentence – Add the prefix	Write the word
Example: He won twenty dollars at the pie-eating __con__test.	contest
Example: My uncle's bakery was the __co__sponsor of the contest.	cosponsor
Example: You have to watch your __con__duct when you are in the public eye.	conduct
1. Luis studied the _____lapse of the Roman Empire last term.	
2. We had to _____pare the book to the movie.	
3. I finally _____pleted the report late last night.	
4. The salt water _____roded the body of Andy's car.	
5. Their _____stant partying drove their roommate crazy.	

Exercise 5 · Find It: Indirect Objects

▸ Listen and follow along as your teacher reads the text below.

▸ Reread the text.

▸ Find and underline each indirect object.

▸ Circle each direct object.

> The rafts drifted slowly down the Nile. They brought the stonecutters the large blocks to cut. These blocks gave workers the material they needed for construction of the pyramids. Slowly and carefully, blocks were cut and placed on top of each other according to a plan. Sometimes mistakes were made. The bosses did not forgive stonecutters their errors. Mistakes would cost men their jobs.
>
> Today, history gives us facts about how the pyramids were made.

Exercise 6 · Identify It: *Have* in Perfect Tense Verbs

▸ Circle the form of **have** in each sentence.

▸ Underline the main verb.

▸ Draw a box around the helping verb **will** if it appears in the sentence.

▸ Fill in the bubble to indicate if the verb is in the past perfect, present perfect, or future perfect tense.

	Past	Present	Future
	Perfect	Perfect	Perfect

1. Kirk has prepared a slide show presentation.
   ○ ○ ○

2. He had chosen this format for his project a long time ago.
   ○ ○ ○

3. Laura had given him help on his slides.
   ○ ○ ○

4. By Thursday all students will have presented their projects.
   ○ ○ ○

5. Kirk has practiced his presentation several times.
   ○ ○ ○

Exercise 7 · Answering Multiple-Choice and Open-Ended Comprehension Questions

▸ Read the following selection and use the selection to answer the questions on the next page.

Four-Footed Hero

On September 11, 2001, terrorists crashed two planes into the World Trade Center in New York City. Hundreds of heroes rushed into the <u>blazing</u> buildings. These brave people were rushing to help victims trapped in the buildings.

Some of the heroes who worked so hard to save people had four feet, rather than two. One of these four-footed heroes was twelve years old. His name was Bear. He was a golden retriever dog. Bear and his owner, Captain Scott Shields, were on scene at the World Trade Center thirty-eight minutes after the first plane struck.

As the first rescue dog on site, Bear went right to work. He used his powerful sense of smell to locate people. He worked twenty-two hours a day for three straight days. Bear never gave up. Only five survivors were found in the <u>debris</u> of the buildings. Bear was responsible for finding three of the five survivors.

Bear received many honors and awards. He was invited to lead a famous parade in New York City. Bear died in 2002. When he died, there was a memorial service to honor him on the *U.S.S. Intrepid*, an aircraft carrier. Bear was a true hero.

(continued)

Exercise 7 (continued) · Answering Multiple-Choice and Open-Ended Comprehension Questions

▸ Read each question and answer choices.

▸ Fill in the bubble for the correct answer.

1. A synonym for the word **blazing** in the second sentence is
   - Ⓐ giant.
   - Ⓑ ruined
   - Ⓒ falling.
   - Ⓓ burning.

2. The word **debris** in the third paragraph most likely refers to the
   - Ⓐ pieces of the destroyed buildings.
   - Ⓑ place where Bear lived.
   - Ⓒ street the buildings were on
   - Ⓓ buildings next to the World Trade Center.

3. Which sentence from the passage tells the reader why Bear is a hero?
   - Ⓐ He was a golden retriever dog.
   - Ⓑ Bear went right to work.
   - Ⓒ Bear was responsible for finding three of the five survivors
   - Ⓓ Bear died in 2002.

4. The title of this passage refers to
   - Ⓐ the people who went into the burning buildings.
   - Ⓑ a dog that rescued people.
   - Ⓒ Captain Scott Shields.
   - Ⓓ the five survivors of the attack.

5. The main idea of this passage is
   - Ⓐ dogs, as well as people, can be heroes.
   - Ⓑ Bear led a famous parade.
   - Ⓒ Bear was a golden retriever.
   - Ⓓ terrorists attacked buildings.

Number Correct _____ /5

(continued)

Exercise 7 (continued) · Answering Multiple-Choice and Open-Ended Comprehension Questions

▶ What can you infer about why Bear was honored with a memorial service? Use the text to help with your answer.

_____

_____

_____

_____

_____

_____

_____

_____

Trait	Point
Ideas/Content	
Organization	
Word Choice	
Sentence Fluency	
Conventions	

Total Number Correct _____ /10

Exercise 1 · Listening for Stressed Syllables

▸ Listen to each word your teacher says. Repeat the word.

▸ Count the syllables. Write the number in the first column.

▸ Listen as your teacher says the word again. Identify the stressed syllable.

▸ Write the letters for the stressed syllable in the correct column.

	How many syllables do you hear?	First Syllable	Second Syllable	Third Syllable
1.				
2.				
3.				
4.				
5.				

Exercise 2 · Sort It: Meaning Categories

▸ Read the words in the **Word Bank**.

▸ Sort the words into categories according to meaning.

▸ Use the text selections **"Living in Egypt"** and **"Growing Up Egyptian"** for context clues about word meaning as needed.

▸ Write each word in the correct column.

Word Bank

Nile River	Hebeny	Thebes	scribe	Egypt
Moses	Memphis	father	September	farmer
today	June	Africa		

People	Places	Time

Lesson Checklist
Lessons 1–2

Check off the activities you complete with each lesson. Evaluate your accomplishments at the end of each lesson. Pay attention to teacher evaluations and comments.

	Unit Objectives (Lessons 1-5)	Lesson 1 (Date:_____)	Lesson 2 (Date:_____)
STEP 1	• Segment syllables in multisyllable words. • Identify stressed syllables in multisyllable words. • Identify closed, open, **r**-controlled, and final silent **e** syllables	❑ Review: Vowels and Consonants	❑ Review: Syllable Types
STEP 2	• Read fluently and spell words with sound-spelling correspondences, syllable types, and prefixes for this and previous units. • Read fluently and spell the **Essential Words**: to, there, answer, their, people, what, too, want, who, two.	❑ Exercise 1: Spelling Pretest 1 ❑ Exercise 2: Sentence Dictation	❑ Exercise 1: Sort It: Syllable Types ❑ Exercise 2: Build It ❑ Exercise 3: Sentence Dictation ❑ Word Fluency 1 ❑ Handwriting Practice
STEP 3	• Use synonyms, antonyms, homophones, and attributes to identify the relationships in analogies. • Use suffixes to form singular, plurals, and possessives with nouns. • Review prefixes.	❑ Explore It ❑ Expression of the Day	❑ Review: Noun Suffixes and Adjective Suffixes ❑ Exercise 4: Identify It: Noun Suffixes ❑ Exercise 5: Identify It: Adjective and Adverb Suffixes ❑ Expression of the Day
STEP 4	• Use **and**, **but**, and **or** in compound sentences. • Review noun categories and functions. • Review helping verbs **be**, **have**, and **do**.	❑ Review: Nouns ❑ Exercise 3: Sort It: Noun Categories ❑ Exercise 4: Find It: Appositives ❑ Review: Noun Functions ❑ Exercise 5: Identify It: Noun Functions	❑ Review: Noun Functions ❑ Exercise 6: Code It: Noun Functions
STEP 5	• Read phrases and passages fluently. • Preview nonfciction reading selection using text features. • Define vocabulary using context-based strategies. • Read and understand informational text.	❑ Exercise 6: Phrase It ❑ Independent Text: **"Life at the Pole"**	❑ Passage Fluency 1 ❑ Exercise 7: Use the Clues: Vocabulary Strategies
STEP 6	• Generate sentences using a six-stage process. • Distinguish fact and opinion statements. • Answer comprehension questions using **explain**, **distinguish**, **infer**, **use**, **describe**, and **contrast**. • Write an informal outline, introductory, body paragraph, and conclusion for an expository (explanatory) essay. • Revise an expository (explanatory) essay.	❑ Masterpiece Sentences: Stages 1–3 ❑ Review: Fact or Opinion?	❑ Using the Six Traits to Revise a Paragraph Exercise 8: Revise It: Using the Six Traits
Self-Evaluation (5 is the highest) **Effort** = I produced my best work. **Participation** = I was actively involved in tasks. **Independence** = I worked on my own.		**Effort:** 1 2 3 4 5 **Participation:** 1 2 3 4 5 **Independence:** 1 2 3 4 5	**Effort:** 1 2 3 4 5 **Participation:** 1 2 3 4 5 **Independence:** 1 2 3 4 5
Teacher Evaluation		**Effort:** 1 2 3 4 5 **Participation:** 1 2 3 4 5 **Independence:** 1 2 3 4 5	**Effort:** 1 2 3 4 5 **Participation:** 1 2 3 4 5 **Independence:** 1 2 3 4 5

Lesson 3 (Date:_____)	Lesson 4 (Date:_____)	Lesson 5 (Date:_____)
❑ Review: Syllable Types	❑ Review: Syllable Types	❑ Review: Syllable Types
❑ Exercise 1: Sort It: Syllable Types ❑ Exercise 2: Build It ❑ Exercise 3: Sentence Dictation ❑ Word Fluency 1	❑ Exercise 1: Sort It: Syllable Types ❑ Exercise 2: Build It, Bank It ❑ Exercise 3: Sentence Dictation ❑ Word Fluency 2	❑ Content Mastery: Spelling Posttest 1
❑ Word Relationships: Synonyms ❑ Draw It: Idioms ❑ Expression of the Day	❑ Exercise 4: Match It: Using Prefixes ❑ Exercise 5: Rewrite It: Verb Tense ❑ Expression of the Day	❑ Multiple Meaning Map, **body** ❑ Draw It: Idioms ❑ Expression of the Day
❑ Review: Helping Verbs: **be**, **have**, and **do** ❑ Exercise 4: Identify It: Main Verb or Helping Verb ❑ Exercise 5: Choose It and Use It: The Verbs **be**, **have**, and **do**	❑ Review: Irregular Verbs ❑ Review: Tense Timeline ❑ Exercise 6: Find It: Irregular Verb Forms ❑ Exercise 7: Rewrite It: Irregular Past Tense	❑ Masterpiece Sentences: All Stages
❑ Instructional Text: **"Mysteries of Antarctica"** Exercise 6: Use the Clues	❑ Prepare to Write: Expository (Explanatory) Essay	❑ Review Content and Ideas for an Expository Essay
❑ Exercise 7: Answer It: Using Signal Words	❑ Organize Information Using an Informal Outline	❑ Write It: Expository Essay ❑ Write It: Body Paragraph
Effort: 1 2 3 4 5 **Participation:** 1 2 3 4 5 **Independence:** 1 2 3 4 5	**Effort:** 1 2 3 4 5 **Participation:** 1 2 3 4 5 **Independence:** 1 2 3 4 5	**Effort:** 1 2 3 4 5 **Participation:** 1 2 3 4 5 **Independence:** 1 2 3 4 5
Effort: 1 2 3 4 5 **Participation:** 1 2 3 4 5 **Independence:** 1 2 3 4 5	**Effort:** 1 2 3 4 5 **Participation:** 1 2 3 4 5 **Independence:** 1 2 3 4 5	**Effort:** 1 2 3 4 5 **Participation:** 1 2 3 4 5 **Independence:** 1 2 3 4 5

Check off the activities you complete with each lesson. Evaluate your accomplishments at the end of each lesson. Pay attention to teacher evaluations and comments.

	Unit Objectives (Lessons 6–10)	Lesson 6 (Date:_____)	Lesson 7 (Date:_____)
STEP 1	• Segment syllables in multisyllable words. • Identify stressed syllables in multisyllable words. • Identify closed, open, **r**-controlled, and final silent **e** syllables • **End-of-Book Content Mastery: Phonemic Awareness and Phonics**	❑ Exercise 1: Syllable Awareness: Segmentation	❑ Review: Stressed Syllables ❑ Exercise 1: Listening for Stressed Syllables
STEP 2	• Read fluently and spell words with sound-spelling correspondences, syllable types, and prefixes for this and previous units. • Read fluently and spell the **Essential Words**: *to, there, answer, their, people, what, too, want, who, two.* • **Progress Indicator: Test of Silent Contextual Reading** • **Progress Indicator: Spelling Inventory**	❑ Exercise 2: Spelling Pretest 2 ❑ Exercise 3: Sort It: Compound Words ❑ Word Fluency 3	❑ Exercise 2: Divide It ❑ Word Fluency 4
STEP 3	• Use synonyms, antonyms, homophones, and attributes to identify the relationships in analogies. • Review prefixes. • **End-of-Book Content Mastery: Vocabulary and Morphology**	❑ Exercise 4: Identify It: Present and Past Participles ❑ Exercise 5: Rewrite It: Present and Past Participles ❑ Expression of the Day	❑ Exercise 3: Match It: Prefixes ❑ Expression of the Day
STEP 4	• Use **and**, **but**, and **or** in compound sentences. • Review noun categories and functions. • Review helping verbs **be**, **have**, and **do**. • **End-of-Book Content Mastery: Grammar and Usage**	❑ Review: Compound Sentences ❑ Exercise 6: Find It: Compound Sentences ❑ Exercise 7: Combine It: Compound Sentences	❑ Review: Compound Sentences ❑ Review: Diagram It ❑ Exercise 4: Diagram It: Compound Sentences
STEP 5	• Read phrases and passages fluently. • Preview nonfciton reading selection using text features. • Define vocabulary using context-based strategies. • Read and understand informational text. • **Progress Indicator: *Language!* Reading Scale**	❑ Independent Text: **"The First Transcontinental Railroad"** Exercise 8: Use the Clues	❑ Review Content and Ideas for an Expository (Explanatory) Essay
STEP 6	• Answer comprehension questions using **explain**, **distinguish**, **infer**, **use**, **describe**, and **contrast**. • Write an informal outline, introductory, body paragraph, and conclusion for an expository (explanatory) essay. • Revise an expository (explanatory) essay. • **Progress Indicator: Writing**	❑ Exercise 9: Answer It: Using Signal Words	❑ Write It: Body Paragraph ❑ Write It: Conclusion
	Self-Evaluation (5 is the highest) **Effort** = I produced my best work. **Participation** = I was actively involved in tasks. **Independence** = I worked on my own.	**Effort:** 1 2 3 4 5 **Participation:** 1 2 3 4 5 **Independence:** 1 2 3 4 5	**Effort:** 1 2 3 4 5 **Participation:** 1 2 3 4 5 **Independence:** 1 2 3 4 5
	Teacher Evaluation	**Effort:** 1 2 3 4 5 **Participation:** 1 2 3 4 5 **Independence:** 1 2 3 4 5	**Effort:** 1 2 3 4 5 **Participation:** 1 2 3 4 5 **Independence:** 1 2 3 4 5

Lesson 8 (Date:_____)	**Lesson 9** (Date:_____)	**Lesson 10** (Date:_____)
		❑ End-of-Book Content Mastery: Phonemic Awareness and Phonics
❑ Progress Indicator: Test of Silent Contextual Reading Fluency (TOSCRF)	❑ Progress Indicator: Test of Written Spelling 4	❑ Content Mastery: Spelling Posttest 2
❑ Exercise 1: Word Relationships: Analogies ❑ Exercise 2: Word Relationships: Word Pairs with Prefixes ❑ Expression of the Day	❑ Exercise 1: Find It: Word Forms ❑ Exercise 2: Choose It and Use It: Prefixes ❑ Expression of the Day	❑ End-of-Book Content Mastery: Vocabulary and Morphology
❑ Masterpiece Sentences: Compound Sentences	❑ Exercise 3: Rewrite It: Compound Sentences	❑ End-of-Book Content Mastery: Grammar and Usage
❑ Oral Presentation of Expository Essays		❑ Progress Indicator: *Language!* Reading Scale
❑ Check It: Review Writer's Checklist ❑ Revise It: Expository (Explanatory) Essay	❑ Progress Indicator: Writing	
Effort: 1 2 3 4 5 **Participation:** 1 2 3 4 5 **Independence:** 1 2 3 4 5	**Effort:** 1 2 3 4 5 **Participation:** 1 2 3 4 5 **Independence:** 1 2 3 4 5	**Effort:** 1 2 3 4 5 **Participation:** 1 2 3 4 5 **Independence:** 1 2 3 4 5
Effort: 1 2 3 4 5 **Participation:** 1 2 3 4 5 **Independence:** 1 2 3 4 5	**Effort:** 1 2 3 4 5 **Participation:** 1 2 3 4 5 **Independence:** 1 2 3 4 5	**Effort:** 1 2 3 4 5 **Participation:** 1 2 3 4 5 **Independence:** 1 2 3 4 5

Exercise 1 · Spelling Pretest 1

▶ Write the words your teacher repeats.

1. _____   6. _____   11. _____

2. _____   7. _____   12. _____

3. _____   8. _____   13. _____

4. _____   9. _____   14. _____

5. _____   10. _____   15. _____

Exercise 2 · Sentence Dictation

▸ Listen to each sentence your teacher says.

▸ Repeat the sentence.

▸ Write it on the line.

▸ Check for sentence signals—capital letters and end punctuation.

1. _____

2. _____

3. _____

4. _____

5. _____

▸ Read the dictated sentences 1–5.

▸ Find the three words that follow the **Doubling Rule**.

▸ Write those three words on the lines.

_____   _____   _____

Exercise 3 · Sort It: Noun Categories

▸ Preview the four categories in the chart below (people, places, things, ideas).

▸ Read the nouns in the **Word Bank**.

▸ Write each noun in the appropriate column.

▸ Review your nouns with your teacher to ensure that they are in the right columns.

Word Bank

scientists	climate	krill	zone
brine	researcher	South Pole	worker
seeds	winter	Antarctica	fossils
mass	shore	engineer	past
ocean	weather	explorer	month

People	Places	Things	Ideas

Exercise 4 · Find It: Appositives

▸ Reread each sentence.

▸ Underline the noun that is an appositive.

▸ Circle the appositive and any modifiers.

▸ Draw an arrow from the circle to the noun that the appositive explains, renames, or identifies.

1. The ship sailed to Antarctica, the frozen continent.

2. It was bringing equipment to Dr. Nolan, a researcher.

3. Dr. Nolan, a botanist, was studying plants.

4. She was studying the effects of temperature variations on lichen, a hardy plant.

5. March, the last Antarctic summer month, would mark the end of her project.

Unit 18 · Lesson 1

Exercise 5 · Identify It: Noun Functions

▶ Read each sentence and study the underlined noun.

▶ Decide if the noun is a **subject, direct object, indirect object, object of a preposition,** or **appositive.**

▶ Fill in the correct bubble.

▶ Do the first sentence with your teacher.

	Subject	Direct Object	Indirect Object	Object of a Preposition	Appositive
1. The South Pole is on <u>Antarctica</u>.	◯	◯	◯	◯	◯
2. <u>Antarctica</u> is the frozen continent.	◯	◯	◯	◯	◯
3. Small plants live on the frozen <u>shore</u>.	◯	◯	◯	◯	◯
4. Whales migrate and eat <u>krill</u>.	◯	◯	◯	◯	◯
5. Scientists gave <u>whales</u> krill.	◯	◯	◯	◯	◯
6. The migrating birds bring <u>seeds</u>.	◯	◯	◯	◯	◯
7. Antarctica can offer <u>us</u> new information.	◯	◯	◯	◯	◯
8. <u>Scientists</u> establish labs in Antarctica.	◯	◯	◯	◯	◯
9. Antarctica was part of the original land mass, <u>Pangea</u>.	◯	◯	◯	◯	◯
10. <u>Fossils</u> have been found in Antarctica.	◯	◯	◯	◯	◯

Exercise 6 · Phrase It

▸ Use a pencil to "scoop" the phrases in each sentence.

▸ Read each sentence as you would speak it.

▸ The first two sentences are done for you.

1. The temperature is less than zero.

2. The wind chill hits the danger zone.

3. It is very dry and cold in Antarctica.

4. Small plants live on the frozen shore.

5. Summer begins in October and ends in March.

6. A few months pass, and the planet tilts.

7. Winter is dark all the time.

8. There is some light in the sky.

9. Light comes from gases.

10. Swirling gases color the sky.

Exercise 1 · Sort It: Syllable Types

▸ Read the syllables in the box.

▸ Sort the syllables by syllable type.

▸ Write each syllable in the appropriate column.

mar	ket
der	er
pet	un
port	trans
stand	car

Closed	r-Controlled

Exercise 2 · Build It

▶ Combine syllables from Exercise 1, **Sort It: Syllable Types**, to build five new words in three minutes.

▶ Write the words on the lines.

▶ Read and compare words with a partner.

_____   _____   _____

_____   _____   _____

Exercise 3 · Sentence Dictation

▶ Listen to each sentence your teacher says.

▶ Repeat the sentence.

▶ Write it on the line.

▶ Check for sentence signals—capital letters and end punctuation.

▶ Follow the **say-trace-repeat** procedure with the **Essential Words** you missed.

1. _____

2. _____

3. _____

4. _____

5. _____

▶ Read the dictated sentences 1–5.

▶ Which three words or phrases answer the question "When?"

▶ Write those three words or phrases on the lines.

_____   _____   _____

Exercise 4 · Identify It: Noun Suffixes

▸ Read each sentence.

▸ Make an **X** in the column to tell if the underlined word is:
A singular noun (just one)
A plural noun (two or more)
A singular possessive noun (just one owner)
A plural possessive noun (two or more owners)

▸ Work through the examples with your teacher.

Sentence	Singular Noun	Plural Noun	Singular Possessive	Plural Possessive
Examples: In 1498, the explorer Vasco Da Gama discovered a new type of <u>bird</u>.	X			
<u>Flocks</u> of these birds jumped in and out of the water and did not fly.		X		
Never before had Vasco <u>Da Gama's</u> men observed such an odd animal.			X	
The <u>birds'</u> shapes were like bowling pins on two webbed feet.				X
1. A penguin has a black <u>back</u> and a white front.				
2. Penguins walk clumsily but swim briskly, using their wings and feet like <u>flippers</u>.				
3. They make <u>nests</u> on land.				
4. A good <u>meal</u> consists of fish and squid.				
5. <u>Penguins'</u> lives have some fun.				

(continued)

Exercise 4 (continued) · Identify It: Noun Suffixes

Sentence	Singular Noun	Plural Noun	Singular Possessive	Plural Possessive
6. After all, they get to slide on <u>patches</u> of snow and ice into the water.				
7. Like every bird, a penguin's life begins in an <u>egg</u>.				
8. The <u>birds</u>' eggs are often laid in sets of two.				
9. If the weather gets too cold, the mother hides the eggs in a fold of skin that stretches over the <u>mother's</u> stomach.				
10. After the <u>chicks</u> hatch, both parents feed them.				

Unit 18 · Lesson 2

Exercise 5 · Identify It: Adjective and Adverb Suffixes

▸ Read each sentence.

▸ Make an X in the column to show if the underlined word is:
A comparative adjective (compares two things)
A superlative adjective (compares three or more things)
An adverb formed from an adjective (often answers the question *how* or *when*)

▸ Work through the examples with your teacher.

Sentences	Comparative Adjective	Superlative Adjective	Adverb from Adjective
Examples: Sharks <u>easily</u> catch young penguin chicks.			X
Penguins are the <u>funniest</u> birds you have ever seen.		X	
The odd-looking bird has an even <u>sillier</u> call; it sounds like a mule or a donkey.	X		
1. On land they appear to be one of the <u>clumsiest</u> animals alive.			
2. In the water they are <u>sleeker</u> than many fish.			
3. Dinners of raw fish and squid do not <u>exactly</u> help penguins to smell like roses.			
4. People would think you were <u>smellier</u> than a skunk if you tried to live and eat like this bird.			
5. In fact, some people say penguins are the <u>smelliest</u> birds of all.			
6. Other people say that they are <u>funnier</u> than any other animal.			
7. Many people <u>really</u> like watching penguins at the zoo.			

(continued)

Exercise 5 (continued) · Identify It: Adjective and Adverb Suffixes

Sentences	Comparative Adjective	Superlative Adjective	Adverb from Adjective
8. <u>Fewer</u> people, however, like the smell of these birds.			
9. Some whales migrate to the <u>coldest</u> continent for krill.			
10. Antarctica's winter is <u>darker</u> than ours.			

Exercise 6 · Code It: Noun Functions

▶ Read the text.

▶ Decide if each underlined noun is a **subject,** a **direct object,** an **object of a preposition,** or an **appositive.**

▶ Write **s** above each subject, **DO** above each direct object, **OP** above each object of a preposition, and **A** above each appositive.

▶ Do the first example with your teacher.

based on "Life at the Pole"

In the <u>summer</u> at the <u>South Pole</u>, <u>days</u> are long. It is never dark.

Thick <u>shades</u> on <u>homes</u> block the <u>sun</u>. These make the <u>rooms</u> dark.

<u>People</u> can then sleep. After a few <u>months</u>, Earth, our <u>planet</u>, tilts.

<u>Winter</u> starts. Only swirling <u>gases</u> light the <u>sky</u>.

Exercise 7 · Use the Clues: Vocabulary Strategies

▸ Read each pair of sentences.

▸ Find each circled pronoun.

▸ Identify the noun that the pronoun replaces and underline it.

▸ Draw an arrow to show the link between the pronoun and the noun it replaces.

▸ Do the first sentence with your teacher.

1. There is some light in the sky. (It) comes from gases.

2. Shades block the sun. (They) make sleep possible.

3. Many countries govern Antarctica. (It) belongs to all of them.

4. People go there to study. (They) want to understand our planet better.

5. This land was not always frozen. At one time (it) was part of a lush forest.

Exercise 8 · Revise It: Using the Six Traits

▶ Listen to your teacher read this paragraph from a personal narrative. Then, review the **Writer's Checklist** on the next pages.

▶ Put a check next to each item the author did correctly.

▶ For each item that is not checked, use the editor's marks to revise the paragraph.

First, the Egyptians used very simple tools to cut the stone blocks for the pyramids. The Egyptans did not have things like electric drills. They could not blast the stone from a mountain with dynamite. Instead, they used wedges. Then they poured water on the wedges. The wedges soaked up the water like a sponge the water made the wedges expand. Amazing! They drove the wooden wedges into the surface of a huge stone. As they expanded, the wedges split the rock. Once each stone was cut, the workers used other tools to cut it into perfect block shapes.

Editor's Marks

∧	add or change text
ℒ	delete text
⌒→	move text
¶	new paragraph
≡	capitalize
/	lowercase
⊙	insert period
◯	check spelling or spell out word

Book C Writer's Checklist

Trait	Did I...?	Unit
Ideas and Content	Expository writing: ❑ Clearly state the topic of the composition ❑ Focus each paragraph on the topic ❑ Include examples, evidence, and/or explanations to develop each paragraph Personal narrative: ❑ Tell a single true story ❑ Include enough description and detail to develop the message/lesson learned	7 7 7 9 9
Organization	Write paragraphs: ❑ Tell things in an order that makes sense ❑ Include all parts of a paragraph Write an expository essay: ❑ Write an introductory paragraph that states the topic and the plan ❑ Use transition topic sentences to connect paragraphs ❑ Write a concluding paragraph that restates the introductory paragraph Write a personal narrative: ❑ Write an introductory paragraph that hints at the message/lesson learned ❑ Write three middle paragraphs that form the beginning, middle, and end of the story ❑ Use story transitions to connect anecdotes/events ❑ Write a concluding paragraph that explains the message/lesson learned	1 6 7 7 8, 14 9 9 9 9
Voice and Audience Awareness	❑ Think about my audience and purpose for writing ❑ Write in a clear and engaging way that makes my audience want to read my work; can my reader "hear" me speaking ❑ Use the word *I* to write about myself	6 6 9
Word Choice	❑ Try to find my own way to say things ❑ Use words that are lively and specific to the content	2 2

(continued)

Book C Writer's Checklist *(continued)*

Trait	Did I...?	Unit
Sentence Fluency	❏ Write complete sentences	1
	❏ Expand some of my sentences by painting the subject and/or predicate	3–18
	❏ Write a compound sentence part or a compound sentence	7–18
	❏ Write a sentence with a direct object	3–18
Conventions	Capitalize words correctly:	
	❏ Capitalize the first word of each sentence	1
	❏ Capitalize proper nouns, including people's names	3
	Punctuate correctly:	
	❏ Put a period or question mark at the end of each sentence	1 2
	❏ Put an apostrophe before the <u>s</u> for a singular possessive noun	11
	❏ Put an apostrophe after the <u>s</u> for a plural possessive noun	7
	❏ Use an apostrophe with contractions	5
	❏ Use a comma after a long adverb phrase at the beginning of a sentence	
	❏ Use a comma to separate the appositive and its modifiers from the rest of the sentence	10–12
	Use grammar correctly:	
	❏ Use the correct verb tense	4
	❏ Make sure the verb agrees with the subject in number	4
	Spell correctly:	
	❏ Spell all **Essential Words** correctly	1–18
	Apply spelling rules	
	❏ The doubling rule (1-1-1)	6
	❏ The drop <u>e</u> rule	10, 16
	❏ The words ending in <u>o</u> preceded by a consonant rule	15
	❏ The change <u>y</u> rule	17

Exercise 1 · Sort It: Syllable Types

▸ Read the syllables in the box.

▸ Sort the syllables by syllable type by writing each syllable in the correct column.

do	tor	er	pre	pen
u	o	vent	na	men

Closed	r-Controlled	Open

Exercise 2 · Build It

▸ Combine syllables from Exercise 1, **Sort It: Syllable Types**, to build five new words in three minutes.

▸ Write the words on the lines.

▸ Read and compare words with a partner.

_____   _____   _____

_____   _____

Exercise 3 · Sentence Dictation

▸ Listen to each sentence your teacher says.

▸ Repeat the sentence.

▸ Write it on the line.

▸ Check for sentence signals—capital letters and end punctuation.

▸ Follow the **say-trace-repeat** procedure with **Essential Words** you missed.

1. _____

2. _____

3. _____

4. _____

5. _____

▸ Read the dictated sentences 1–5.

▸ Which two words follow the **Change It Rule**? Write those two words on the lines.

_____   _____

Exercise 4 · Identify It: Main Verb or Helping Verb

▸ Read each sentence.

▸ Underline the verb or verb phrase in each sentence.

▸ Decide if **be**, **have**, or **do** is used as a main verb or a helping verb.

▸ Fill in the correct bubble.

	Main Verb	Helping Verb
1. The sun has set over the frozen land.	◯	◯
2. The seawater is cold.	◯	◯
3. Large icebergs have formed in the sea.	◯	◯
4. Scientists will be studying the diverse plants.	◯	◯
5. Some plants do live on the frozen shore.	◯	◯
6. The penguins were on the iceberg.	◯	◯
7. Whales will be looking for krill next summer.	◯	◯
8. The scientists did many tests in their labs.	◯	◯
9. The long winter has brought dark days and nights.	◯	◯
10. Different animals are out on the icebergs.	◯	◯

Exercise 5 · Choose It and Use It: The Verbs *Be, Have,* and *Do*

▸ Read each sentence.

▸ Choose the correct form of the verb under the blank, using the helping verb chart in the *Student Text.*

▸ Fill in the blank with the correct form of the verb.

▸ Do the first sentence with your teacher.

1. Yesterday the sun _____ rise for the first time in several months.
   do

2. Next summer the whales _____ returning to Antarctica.
   be

3. Scientists _____ studied the plant life of this frozen zone.
   have

4. Penguins _____ strange black and white birds.
   be

5. Whales _____ tails with two large flukes.
   have

Unit 18 · Lesson 3

Exercise 6 · Use the Clues: Vocabulary Strategies

1. Work with your teacher to use word substitutions and context cues to define **climate**.

   Antarctica is very dry, cold, and windy. It has the harshest climate, or weather conditions, of all the continents. Most of it is never above freezing.

2. Use context cues to define the word **aurora**.
   - Underline the unfamiliar word.
   - Read the text surrounding the word.
   - Double underline any context cues you can find.

   ---

   based on "Mysteries of Antarctica"

   In Antarctica, the seasons are different. They are reversed from the Northern Hemisphere. Summer lasts from October to March. Winter lasts from April to September. In the middle of summer, daylight lasts 24 hours a day. In the middle of winter, it remains dark all day. In the dark winter months, there is often an aurora display. Green, orange, and red clouds of gas flash across the sky.

   ---

3. Define **aurora** in your own words:

   _____

   _____

   _____

4. Verify your definition with a dictionary or an online reference source.

Exercise 7 · Answer It: Using Signal Words

▶ Read each item and underline each signal word you find.

▶ Think about what the signal word requires you to do.

▶ Then answer the question.

1. Explain why Antarctica is considered a mysterious continent.

   _____

   _____

   _____

   _____

   _____

2. Distinguish between the seasons in Antarctica and the seasons in your hometown.

   _____

   _____

   _____

   _____

   _____

3. Infer what would happen to the sea life in Antarctica if algae were no longer able to grow there.

   _____

   _____

   _____

   _____

   _____

(continued)

4. Explain why scientists search for meteorites in Antarctica.

_____

_____

_____

_____

5. Was Antarctica ever connected to other continents? Explain. Is it connected now? Explain.

_____

_____

_____

_____

Exercise 1 · Sort It: Syllable Types

▸ Read the syllables in the box.

▸ Sort the syllables by syllable type.

▸ Write each syllable in the correct column.

fe	base	line	fume	ver
per	flate	sis	in	ter

Closed	r-Controlled	Open	Final Silent e

Unit 18 · Lesson 4

Exercise 2 · Build It

▸ Combine syllables from Exercise 1, **Sort It: Syllable Types,** to build five new words in three minutes.

▸ Write the words on the lines.

▸ Read and compare words with a partner.

_____   _____   _____

_____   _____   _____

Exercise 3 · Sentence Dictation

▸ Listen to each sentence your teacher says.

▸ Repeat the sentence.

▸ Write it on the line.

▸ Check for sentence signals—capital letters, commas, and end punctuation.

▸ Follow the **say-trace-repeat** procedure with the **Essential Words** you missed.

1. _____

2. _____

3. _____

4. _____

5. _____

▸ Read the dictated sentences 1–5.

▸ Which three words follow the **Drop e Rule**?

▸ Write those three words on the lines.

_____   _____   _____

Exercise 4 · Match It: Using Prefixes

▶ Use what you know about the prefixes to match each word with the definition of its prefix.

▶ Draw a line to connect the word with its definition.

▶ Use a dictionary to verify answers.

Word	Definition
1. indoors	**a.** not
2. distrust	**b.** below
3. underwater	**c.** between, among
4. nonsense	**d.** into
5. interstate	**e.** away, apart

▶ Use the words with prefixes to complete these activities.

▶ Complete the sentences:

    6. A large road that goes between states is a(n) _____ .

    7. The opposite of being above water is being _____ .

▶ Complete the antonym pairs:

    8. sense : _____

    9. outdoors : _____

    10. trust : _____

Unit 18 · Lesson 4

Exercise 5 · Rewrite It: Verb Tense

▸ Review the **Tense Timeline** with your teacher.

Yesterday	Today	Tomorrow
Past	**Present**	**Future**

▸ Use suffixes to change the verb in the first column below to the indicated tense. Write the verb in the blank.

▸ Use the **Doubling** and **Drop e Rules** when necessary.

▸ Read the sentence quietly to check your work.

Verb	Tense	Sentence
Examples		
glide	present progressive	Christopher Columbus and his men _are gliding_ in three ships to the continent, America.
help	past	The Queen of Spain ___helped___ Columbus pay for the three ships.
enter	present	Columbus ___enters___ an unexplored part of the sea.
1. spot	present	When a sailor _____ a pelican, he shouts out with joy.
2. say	present progressive	Columbus _____ that pelicans mean land is nearby.
3. pluck	future	A few days later they _____ a branch from the water.
4. land	past	At two o'clock in the morning, October 12, 1492, they _____ on a small island.
5. swim	present	People _____ to the boat to bring gifts to Columbus and his men.

Exercise 6 · Find It: Irregular Verb Forms

▸ Read each sentence.

▸ Underline the past tense verb.

▸ Write the past, present, and future forms of the verb in the chart below the **Tense Timeline** on the next page.

1. The storm clouds flew overhead.

2. During the summer the days became very long.

3. Scientists did all their work out on the icebergs.

4. The sun began its slow drop below the horizon.

5. During the winter, the whales went north to warmer waters.

6. The buildings withstood the strong winds.

7. In the dark, the men mistook one machine for another.

8. Scientists brought their equipment to Antarctica.

9. The frozen land shone in the sun.

10. Once, Antarctica had abundant life on it.

(continued)

Unit 18 · Lesson 4

Exercise 6 (continued) · Find It: Irregular Verb Forms

	Yesterday	Today	Tomorrow
	Past	Present	Future

	Irregular Past Tense	Present Tense	Future Tense
1.			
2.			
3.			
4.			
5.			
6.			
7.			
8.			
9.			
10.			

Exercise 7 · Rewrite It: Irregular Past Tense

▸ Read each sentence.

▸ Underline the verb.

▸ Rewrite the sentence, changing the verb to the past tense.

▸ Check for sentence signals—capital letters, commas, and end punctuation.

1. The scientists lend their equipment to each other.

_____

_____

2. The experiment begins in the lab.

_____

_____

3. The iceberg becomes separated from the main pack.

_____

_____

4. In winter the birds fly north to warmer land.

_____

_____

5. During the winter the scientists do their work indoors.

_____

_____

Exercise 1 · Syllable Awareness: Segmentation

▸ Listen to the word.

▸ Count the syllables. Write the number in the first column.

▸ Write the letter for each vowel sound you hear.

▸ Mark the vowel with a diacritical mark.

	How many syllables do you hear?	First vowel sound	Second vowel sound	Third vowel sound
1.				
2.				
3.				
4.				
5.				
6.				
7.				
8.				
9.				
10.				

Exercise 2 · Spelling Pretest 2

▶ Write the words your teacher repeats.

1. _____   6. _____   11. _____

2. _____   7. _____   12. _____

3. _____   8. _____   13. _____

4. _____   9. _____   14. _____

5. _____   10. _____   15. _____

Exercise 3 · Sort It: Compound Words

▶ Sort the words into categories.

▶ Record words on the chart.

Word Bank

brother	dateline	clockwork	exploring	tornado
outside	pathway	sunset	translate	antilock

Compound Words	Not Compound Words

Exercise 4 · Identify It: Present and Past Participles

▸ Read each phrase below.

▸ Underline the participle.

▸ Put an X in the correct column to show if the phrase contains a present participle or a past participle.

Phrase	Phrase Contains Present Participle	Phrase Contains Past Participle
1. An exciting ride		
2. A respected woman explorer		
3. A well-prepared meal		
4. Buzzing insects		
5. An unexplored land		
6. the connecting landmasses		
7. working parents		
8. explored territory		
9. a melting iceberg		
10. an extended offer		

Exercise 5 · Rewrite It: Present and Past Participles

▸ Change the verb to the type of participle that best fits the meaning of the sentence.

▸ Read the sentences quietly to check your work.

Verb	Sentence
Examples: complete	The _**completed**_ railroad connected the East and West Coasts.
laugh	A happy, _**laughing**_ crowd gathered to witness the event.
1. excite	The _____ children ran back and forth.
2. swing	_____ hammers struck metal.
3. yell	_____ reporters pushed themselves to the front of the crowd.
4. dedicate	The _____ workers had constructed long lines of track across America.
5. finish	The _____ railroad would connect the two sides of the continent.

Exercise 6 · Find It: Compound Sentences

▸ Read each compound sentence.

▸ Find the two complete sentences in each compound sentence and underline them.

▸ Circle the conjunction.

1. Fossils have been discovered, and even bits of Mars have been found.

2. Antarctica is now a frozen land, but at one time it was a lush forest.

3. Scientists can work outdoors, or they can work in the lab.

4. Many countries govern Antarctica, and they decide on new rules together.

5. The winter nights are cold and dark, but the summer days are sunny and long.

Exercise 7 · Combine It: Compound Sentences

▶ Read each sentence pair.

▶ Decide whether to use the conjunction **and**, **but**, or **or** to join the sentences.

▶ Write the new compound sentence on the line.

▶ Circle the conjunction you used to join the sentences.

▶ Check for sentence signals—capital letters, commas, and end punctuation.

1. Huge waves crashed onto the iceberg.
   The water froze instantly.

   _____

   _____

2. Scientists find the long Antarctic night challenging.
   They still continue with their work.

   _____

   _____

3. The whales should swim north at the end of the summer.
   They will be trapped in the ice.

   _____

   _____

4. It is hard to sleep in the daylight.
   Shades make the rooms dark.

   _____

   _____

5. Scientists set up labs on the frozen continent.
   They study the thinning ozone.

   _____

   _____

Exercise 8 · Use the Clues Vocabulary Strategies

1. Work with your teacher to use substitution to define **locomotive**.

   Two locomotives idle on their tracks. The two engines of the trains sit nose to nose.

2. Use substitution to define **transported**.
   - Underline the unfamiliar word.
   - Read the text surrounding the unfamiliar word.
   - Look for a word that substitutes for the unfamiliar word. (Hint: the substitution clue may come before or after the unfamiliar word.)
   - Double underline the substitution clue.
   - Draw an arrow from the underlined term **transported** to the definition.

   ---

   based on "The First Transcontinental Railroad"

   The Union Pacific had its own problems. At first, it shipped supplies and equipment up the Missouri River by steamboat and then transported them overland by stagecoach and in wagons. Later, supplies were sent along tracks already laid. But this was slow. It took the labor of thousands to complete this incredible transcontinental task.

   ---

3. Define **transported** in your own words:

   _____

   _____

4. Verify your definition of the word **transported** by using a dictionary reference source.

Exercise 9 · Answer It: Using Signal Words

▸ Read each item and underline each signal word you find.

▸ Think about what the signal word requires you to do.

▸ Then answer the question.

1. Both the Central Pacific and the Union Pacific had problems getting supplies to workers. Distinguish between the ways the two companies had supplies shipped to them.

_____

_____

_____

_____

_____

_____

_____

2. Use a T-chart to show differences between the Union Pacific Railroad workers and the Central Pacific Railroad workers.

Union Pacific Railroad workers	Central Pacific Railroad workers

(continued)

3. Describe the living conditions for the railroad workers.

_____

_____

_____

_____

_____

_____

4. What can you infer from the fact that no Chinese workers were included in the photograph taken at the completion of the railroad?

_____

_____

_____

_____

_____

_____

5. Contrast the mood conveyed by the author in the first two paragraphs of the selection with the mood conveyed in the last paragraph.

_____

_____

_____

_____

_____

_____

Exercise 1 · Listening for Stressed Syllables

▶ Listen to the word your teacher says.

▶ Repeat the word.

▶ Listen for the stressed, or accented, syllable.

▶ Put an X in the box to mark the position of the stressed syllable.

	First syllable	Second syllable	Third syllable
1. again			
2. tomorrow			
3. together			
4. alone			
5. certain			

Exercise 2 · Divide It

▶ Read each sentence silently.

▶ Use the steps of **Divide It** to break each boldface word into syllables.

▶ Blend the syllables together to read each word.

▶ After dividing, read the sentences to a partner.

Two **locomotives** idled on their tracks. Thousands **labored** to **connect** the tracks. What an **amazing** task!

locomotives   labored   connect   amazing

Exercise 3 · Match It: Prefixes

▸ Use what you know about the prefixes to match each word with the definition of its prefix.

▸ Draw a line to connect the prefixed word with the definition of the prefix.

▸ Use a dictionary to verify answers.

Words with Prefixes	Definitions of Prefixes
1. substandard	a. across, beyond
2. transport	b. below
3. preboard	c. before
4. antitoxin	d. with
5. concert	e. against

▸ Write a prefix or a word with a prefix to complete the sentences.

6. Families with small children can board the airplane before others; they

_____ the plane.

7. After a snake bit him, the child was given an _____ .

8. The band played well together, and everyone enjoyed the wonderful

_____ .

9. Planes were used to _____ the equipment to the Antarctic.

10. She didn't want to work for _____ pay.

Exercise 4 · Diagram It: Compound Sentences

▸ Read each sentence.

▸ Find the two complete sentences and underline them.

▸ Circle the conjunction.

▸ Diagram the sentence.

▸ Do the first example with your teacher.

1. Scientists study the ozone layer, and they conduct many experiments.

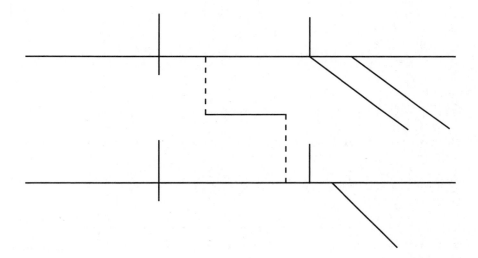

(continued)

Exercise 4 *(continued)* • **Diagram It: Compound Sentences**

2. Some ice melts at the South Pole, and the water level rises.

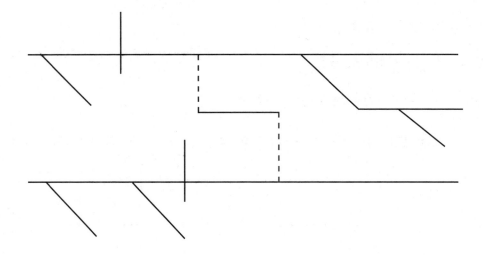

3. The penguins nest during the summer, but they leave the ice cap in winter.

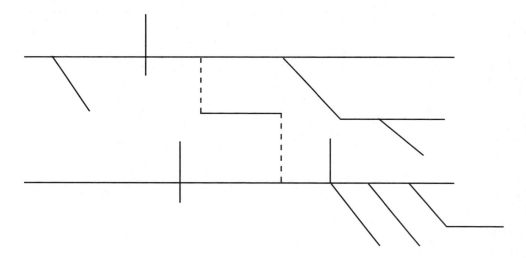

(continued)

Exercise 4 (continued) · Diagram It: Compound Sentences

4. The summer sun shines for long hours, but in winter the sun does not rise.

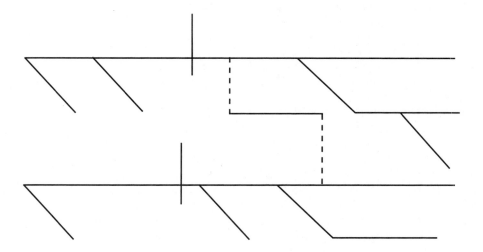

5. Scientists find fossils, and they learn details about earlier life.

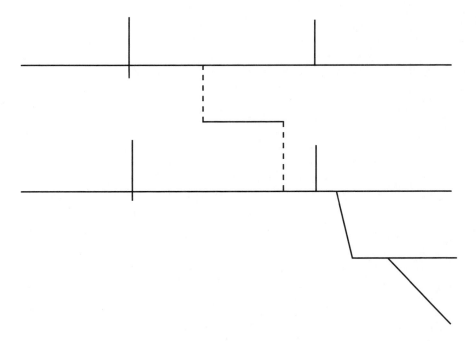

Exercise 1 · Word Relationships: Analogies

▸ Read the word pairs.

▸ Identify the relationship between the words.

▸ Write another pair of words that shows that same relationship.

▸ Use the example as a model.

Example: sunset : end

sunrise : beginning

1. eye : look _____

2. before : after _____

3. continent : land _____

4. locate : find _____

5. number : math _____

Exercise 2 · Word Relationships: Word Pairs with Prefixes

▸ Read the word pairs.

▸ Think about the meaning of the prefix in both words.

▸ Fill in the bubble that matches the meaning of the prefix.

▸ Do the example with your teacher.

Example: Listen: **subway : submarine**

What does the prefix in this word pair mean?

subway : submarine

    Ⓐ over

    Ⓑ below

    Ⓒ against

Fill in the bubble for **below**. The prefix **sub-** means **under** or **below**.

▸ Finish the remaining items independently.

1. anti-drug : anti-war

    Ⓐ against

    Ⓑ opposite

    Ⓒ into

2. predate : preshrunk

    Ⓐ with

    Ⓑ across

    Ⓒ before

3. interact : interstate

    Ⓐ over

    Ⓑ between

    Ⓒ apart

4. redo : refinish

    Ⓐ again

    Ⓑ over

    Ⓒ not

5. unexplored : unopened

    Ⓐ again

    Ⓑ over

    Ⓒ not

Exercise 1 · Find It: Word Forms

▸ Read the word form.

▸ Read the sentence.

▸ Underline the word in the sentence that shows the form named in the first column.

▸ Do the examples with your teacher.

Form	Sentence
Examples: Singular possessive	Some people call the continent of Antarctica a penguin's playground.
Past participle	Others call it a frozen frontier of snow and ice.
Singular present tense verb	In the center of the continent stands the South Pole.
Singular noun	It isn't a real vertical pole, of course.
Appositive	The first person to reach the South Pole was a daring explorer, Roald Amundsen.
1. Adverb made from adjective	On January 15, 1911, his men quickly began to set up a base camp on the continent of Antarctica.
2. Compound word	Nine strong dogs pulled each dogsled from the boat to the camp.
3. Past tense verb	Moving ten tons of supplies a day, the sled dogs helped the workers immensely.
4. Past participle	From the fully stocked base camp, Amundsen, four other men, and four dogsleds began the trek to the pole on October 14.
5. Plural possessive	Gliding over the ice, the dogsleds' progress was at first very rapid.

(continued)

Exercise 1 (continued) · Find It: Word Forms

Form	Sentence
6. Comparative adjective	Soon a much harder part of the trip began; the group had to cross a huge glacier.
7. Adverb made from adjective	The men finally crossed the glacier and again began rapid travel.
8. Plural noun	Once again the dogs moved quickly across the snow.
9. Past tense	Amundsen worried that another explorer, Robert Scott, might beat him to the pole.
10. Superlative adjective	On December 14, 1911, Roald Amundsen and the four others became the happiest people on the planet; they reached the South Pole.

Unit 18 · Lesson 9

Exercise 2 · Choose It and Use It: Prefixes

▶ Read each pair of sentences.

▶ Look at the underlined word in the first sentence.

▶ Choose the prefix from the **Word Bank** that has the same meaning as that word, and write the prefix in the blank in the second sentence.

▶ Reread the second sentence with the newly created word.

Word Bank

pre	trans	inter	sub	anti	super

1. In 1869 the first railroad <u>across</u> the country was completed. It was America's

   first _____ continental railroad.

2. The child did not have the strength to fight <u>against</u> the infection. The doctors

   used an _____ toxin to stop the illness.

3. There was a discussion <u>between</u> two students in the class. It was an interesting

   _____ change.

4. Much is known about events that happened even <u>before</u> history was recorded.

   Fossils can tell us about _____ historic times.

5. Temperatures in the Antarctic are usually <u>below</u> freezing. They are

   _____ zero temperatures.

Exercise 3 · Rewrite It: Compound Sentences

▸ Read the text with your teacher.

▸ Reread each underlined sentence pair.

▸ Use a conjunction (**and, or, but**) to combine the underlined sentences into a compound sentence.

▸ Write the new compound sentence on the numbered line on the next page.

▸ Check for sentence signals—capital letters, commas, and end punctuation.

▸ Reread the new paragraph with your teacher.

---

adapted from "Mysteries of Antarctica"

<u>Antarctica is mountainous. It is cold, dry, and windy.</u> Some plants
        1
and animals such as krill live in the ocean there. <u>Krill are very small.</u>
                                                       2
<u>They provide food for the largest mammal.</u> <u>Many whales migrate</u>
        2   3
<u>to Antarctica in summer. They eat the krill there.</u> As the winter
        3
begins, the large animals and birds leave the Antarctic area. <u>That</u>
                                                                 4
<u>whale should swim north. It could be trapped in the ice!</u> The tiny
        4
life forms stay behind. They live inside the sea ice. <u>They wait for</u>
                                                        5
<u>summer to start again.</u>
        5

(continued)

Exercise 3 (continued) · Rewrite It: Compound Sentences

1. _____

_____

Some plants and animals such as krill can survive there. **2.** _____

_____

_____

3. _____

_____

As the winter begins, the large animals and birds leave. **4.** _____

_____

_____

The tiny life forms stay behind. **5.** _____

_____

_____

Resources

Vowel Chart

Vowel Chart

| ē | ĭ | ā | ě | ă | ī | ŏ | ŭ | aw | ō | ŏŏ | ōō |

ē — these
1. these
2. _____
3. _____
4. _____
5. _____
6. _____
7. _____
8. _____

ĭ — sit
1. sit
2. _____
3. _____

ā — make
1. make
2. _____
3. _____
4. _____
5. _____
6. _____
7. _____
8. _____
9. _____

ě — pet
1. pet
2. _____

ă — cat
1. cat

ī — time
1. _____
2. time
3. _____
4. _____
5. _____

ŏ — fox
1. fox
2. _____
3. _____
4. _____
5. _____
6. _____

ŭ — cup
1. cup
2. _____
3. _____
4. dog
5. _____

aw — dog
1. _____
2. vote
3. _____
4. _____
5. _____
6. _____
7. _____

ō — vote
1. _____
2. put
3. _____
4. _____
5. _____
6. _____
7. _____
8. _____

ŏŏ — put
1. _____
2. _____
3. tube
4. _____
5. _____
6. _____

ōō — tube

Consonant Chart

Mouth Position

Type of Consonant Sound	Lips	Lips/Teeth	Tongue Between Teeth	Tongue Behind Teeth	Roof of Mouth	Back of Mouth	Throat
Stops	/ b / / p /			/ t / / d /		/ k / / g /	
Fricatives		/ f / / v /	/ th / / tẖ /	/ s / / z /	/ sh /		/ h /
Affricatives					/ j / / ch /		
Nasals	/ m /			/ n /		/ ng /	
Lateral				/ l /			
Semivowels	/ w / / hw /			/ r /	/ y /		

English Consonant Chart based on Bolinger, D. (1975). *Aspects of Language* (2nd ed.) (p. 41). New York: Harcourt Brace Jovanovich.

Divide It Checklist

Steps for Syllable Division	Example: disconnected
First, check the word for prefixes and suffixes. Circle them. Next, look at the rest of the word:	(dis)connect(ed)
1. Underline the **first** vowel. Write a **v** under it.	(dis)connect(ed) v̄
2. Underline the **next** vowel. Write a **v** under it.	(dis)connect(ed) v̄ v̄
3. Look at the letters **between** the vowels. Mark them with a **c** for consonant.	(dis)connect(ed) v̄cc v̄
4. Look at the pattern and divide according to the pattern.	(dis)con/nect(ed) v̄cc v̄
5. Place a diacritical mark over the vowels. Cross out the **e** at the end of final silent **e** syllables. Listen for schwa in the unaccented syllable, cross out the vowel, and place a ə symbol above it.	(dis)cŏn/nĕct(ed) v̄cc v̄
Finally, blend each syllable and read the word.	disconnected

Diacritical Marks and Symbols

Diacritical marks and **symbols** are used to indicate the correct sound for the vowel graphemes.

breve / brĕv /	ă	short vowel phonemes
macron	ā	long vowel phonemes
circumflex	âr	**r**-controlled phonemes
schwa	ə	schwa phoneme

Syllable Division Patterns

Pattern	How to Divide	Examples
vccv	vc / cv • Divide between the consonants. • The first syllable is closed. • The vowel sound is short.	năp/kĭn VCCV
vcv	v/cv • **Usually**, divide after the first vowel. • The first syllable is open. • The vowel sound is long. **Note:** If the first vowel is followed by an **r**, the syllable is **r**-controlled. or vc/v • If the first division does not result in a recognizable word, divide after the consonant. • The first syllable is closed. • The vowel sound is short.	sī/lənt VCV mâr/kĕt V CV nĕv/êr VCV
vcccv	• vc/ccv or vcc/cv • Divide before or after the blend or digraph. • Do not split the blend or digraph.	ăth/lēte VCCCV
vv	• v/v • Divide between the vowels if they are not a vowel team or diphthong. • The first syllable is open. • The vowel sound is long.	nē/ŏn VV
c + le	• /cle • Count back three and divide.	crā/dle 321

Book C Writer's Checklist

Trait	Did I...?	Unit
Ideas and Content	Expository writing: ❏ Clearly state the topic of the composition ❏ Focus each paragraph on the topic ❏ Include examples, evidence, and/or explanations to develop each paragraph Personal narrative: ❏ Tell a single true story ❏ Include enough description and detail to develop the message/lesson learned	7 7 7 9 9
Organization	Write paragraphs: ❏ Tell things in an order that makes sense ❏ Include all parts of a paragraph Write an expository essay: ❏ Write an introductory paragraph that states the topic and the plan ❏ Use transition topic sentences to connect paragraphs ❏ Write a concluding paragraph that restates the introductory paragraph Write a personal narrative: ❏ Write an introductory paragraph that hints at the message/lesson learned ❏ Write three middle paragraphs that form the beginning, middle, and end of the story ❏ Use story transitions to connect anecdotes/events ❏ Write a concluding paragraph that explains the message/lesson learned	1 6 7 7 8, 14 9 9 9 9
Voice and Audience Awareness	❏ Think about my audience and purpose for writing ❏ Write in a clear and engaging way that makes my audience want to read my work; can my reader "hear" me speaking ❏ Use the word *I* to write about myself	6 6 9
Word Choice	❏ Try to find my own way to say things ❏ Use words that are lively and specific to the content	2 2

Book C Writer's Checklist *(continued)*

Trait	Did I...?	Unit
Sentence Fluency	❑ Write complete sentences	1
	❑ Expand some of my sentences by painting the subject and/or predicate	3–18
	❑ Write a compound sentence part or a compound sentence	7–18
	❑ Write a sentence with a direct object	3–18
Conventions	Capitalize words correctly:	
	❑ Capitalize the first word of each sentence	1
	❑ Capitalize proper nouns, including people's names	3
	Punctuate correctly:	
	❑ Put a period or question mark at the end of each sentence	1
		2
	❑ Put an apostrophe before the **s** for a singular possessive noun	11
	❑ Put an apostrophe after the **s** for a plural possessive noun	7
	❑ Use an apostrophe with contractions	5
	❑ Use a comma after a long adverb phrase at the beginning of a sentence	
	❑ Use a comma to separate the appositive and its modifiers from the rest of the sentence	10–12
	Use grammar correctly:	
	❑ Use the correct verb tense	4
	❑ Make sure the verb agrees with the subject in number	4
	Spell correctly:	
	❑ Spell all **Essential Words** correctly	1–18
	Apply spelling rules	
	❑ The doubling rule (1-1-1)	6
	❑ The drop **e** rule	10, 16
	❑ The words ending in **o** preceded by a consonant rule	15
	❑ The change **y** rule	17

Word Fluency 1

	Correct	Errors
1st Try		
2nd Try		

#										
10	vanish	finish	punish	prison	salad	second	seven	select	melon	lemon
20	melon	prison	lemon	salad	second	finish	select	vanish	punish	seven
30	lemon	seven	second	vanish	melon	salad	punish	prison	finish	select
40	prison	punish	seven	select	finish	lemon	salad	melon	vanish	second
50	salad	lemon	prison	second	seven	punish	vanish	finish	select	melon
60	select	second	melon	finish	lemon	vanish	finish	select	seven	prison
70	punish	vanish	second	seven	select	lemon	prison	vanish	lemon	salad
80	lemon	salad	finish	vanish	select	prison	lemon	select	salad	melon
90	finish	second	vanish	melon	select	seven	melon	lemon	prison	punish
100	vanish	finish	punish	prison	salad	second	seven	select	melon	lemon

Word Fluency 2

	Correct	Errors
1st Try		
2nd Try		

compact	complex	conduct	conflict	construct	consult	contact	content	subject	suspect	10
conflict	content	suspect	conduct	subject	construct	consult	compact	contact	complex	20
conduct	subject	contact	content	consult	complex	suspect	construct	conflict	compact	30
construct	consult	complex	suspect	compact	subject	conduct	conflict	content	contact	40
suspect	conduct	subject	complex	content	conflict	construct	contact	compact	consult	50
contact	conflict	content	consult	suspect	compact	subject	complex	construct	conduct	60
consult	complex	compact	subject	contact	conduct	conflict	construct	suspect	content	70
complex	conduct	conflict	contact	construct	suspect	content	subject	consult	compact	80
content	contact	consult	complex	conflict	conduct	compact	suspect	construct	subject	90
compact	complex	conduct	conflict	construct	consult	contact	content	subject	suspect	100

Word Fluency 3

	Correct	Errors
1st Try		
2nd Try		

10	disconnect	uncommon	unplug	unlock	nonstop	nonfat	invent	disrupt
20	distinct	unlock	disrupt	nonstop	nonfat	uncommon	instruct	invent
30	disrupt	invent	nonfat	disconnect	distinct	nonstop	unplug	instruct
40	unlock	unplug	invent	instruct	uncommon	disrupt	invent	nonfat
50	nonstop	disrupt	unlock	nonfat	invent	unplug	instruct	disconnect
60	instruct	nonfat	distinct	uncommon	disrupt	disconnect	invent	unlock
70	unplug	disconnect	nonfat	invent	instruct	nonfat	disrupt	nonstop
80	disrupt	nonstop	uncommon	unplug	uncommon	disconnect	instruct	distinct
90	uncommon	nonfat	disconnect	distinct	instruct	invent	unlock	unplug
100	disconnect	uncommon	unplug	unlock	nonstop	nonfat	invent	disrupt

Word Fluency 4

	Correct	Errors
1st Try		
2nd Try		

gone	look	water	most	see	people	most	gone	water	people	10
look	see	people	gone	look	most	water	see	most	look	20
gone	people	see	people	gone	look	most	water	people	see	30
water	people	most	see	look	most	see	gone	water	people	40
look	look	water	see	people	water	look	see	people	most	50
gone	water	gone	look	most	see	most	people	water	gone	60
most	look	water	gone	see	water	most	gone	water	people	70
look	look	see	water	people	gone	people	look	see	water	80
people	look	most	see	look	water	water	people	most	gone	90
water	water	gone	look	people	most	see	water	look	most	100

Passage Fluency 1

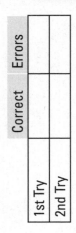

Correct	Errors	
		1st Try
		2nd Try

Some inventions are made just for fun. Some of 9
them are odd, and many of them have odd names. 19
What do we call inventions like these? They are 28
"off-the-wall." They are just not useful, so not many of 38
them will sell. They will not have any impact, but they 49
are not supposed to! Many "off-the-wall" inventions 56
have become fads. A fad is a quick craze. Fads become 67
the rage, and people like them. Fads are fun, but not 78
for long. 80

Do you know someone who comes up with 88
"off-the-wall" inventions? Meet Mr. Robinson. He 94
has thought of lots of nutty things. One of his crazy 105
inventions stretches pasta! Another one puts a 112
square peg in a round hole! How useful is that? Are 123
you impressed? No, but you are amused. That's why 132
Mr. Robinson invents this nutty stuff. He just loves 141
tinkering, and he loves odd things. Mr. Robinson is 150
the king of "off-the-wall" inventions! 155

Step back in time to 1985. In England, a man is 166
making a small three-wheeled bike. This bike isn't 174
ridden, it's driven! It's called the C5, and it runs on 185
batteries, not gas. It emits no gas fumes. Some ships 195
have used the C5 because the small C5s can drive 205
across the decks of big ships. A C5 helps move things 216
on a ship. But there is a problem. If you drive the C5 229
in traffic, you'll find that it's too small and sluggish. 239
The driver is too exposed. Passing cars emit gas 248
fumes, and drivers inhale the fumes! 254

	Correct	Errors
1st Try		
2nd Try		

What makes an inventor? Inventors have quick 7
minds. They think about problems, and they come 15
up with solutions. Many inventions impact our lives 23
by making our lives better. Lots of us have ideas and 34
think about things. If you have an invention, you 43
should get a patent, which says that your invention 52
belongs to you. It stops others from robbing your 61
idea. 62

Inventors begin with a problem and think about it. 71
They think of possible solutions. This is how they 80
may think about cars. For example, most cars use too 90
much gas. The gas makes fumes and pollution. Think 99
about these problems. What if you could make a car 109
that pollutes less? Is it possible that a car can use less 121
gas? Is that possible? It is, and here is one solution. 132

Make a car of plastic; that could solve it. The car 143
wouldn't be as heavy, so it would use less gas. It 154
would pollute less, too. Plastic lasts and doesn't rust, 163
and the color doesn't fade. There would be a bonus, 173
as well, since plastic is manmade, and it can be 183
reused. Think of all the juice we drink that comes in 194
plastic jugs. We could use the same plastic to make 204
more cars. Is plastic the answer to making better 213
cars? Many think so. 217

Word Fluency 1

	Correct	Errors
1st Try		
2nd Try		

10	barn	barber	bar	spark	park	part	start	star	farm	far
20	barber	barn	part	start	farm	star	bar	far	spark	park
30	barn	part	barber	park	bar	spark	far	star	farm	start
40	spark	bar	part	barn	star	farm	start	barber	park	far
50	bar	farm	barn	barber	spark	start	star	far	part	park
60	star	far	bar	start	park	barn	barber	spark	farm	part
70	barber	barn	far	barn	star	part	farm	part	bar	spark
80	park	spark	bar	park	barn	star	start	farm	barber	far
90	spark	bar	barber	park	spark	park	star	start	farm	part
100	far	part	barn	spark	farm	barber	park	bar	start	star

Word Fluency 2

	Correct	Errors
1st Try		
2nd Try		

interpret	interact	understand	underpass	interest	understand	perhaps	person	permit	pepper	10
underbrush	perhaps	interpret	person	understand	interact	underpass	pepper	interest	permit	20
underpass	interact	understand	interpret	person	underbrush	permit	interest	permit	pepper	30
interpret	underbrush	permit	understand	interact	perhaps	pepper	interest	pepper	perhaps	40
underbrush	interest	understand	interact	perhaps	person	permit	pepper	interest	person	50
interest	interpret	understand	underpass	underbrush	perhaps	understand	person	interpret	understand	60
perhaps	interact	interest	pepper	interact	understand	underbrush	interpret	pepper	permit	70
interpret	permit	interact	underpass	understand	interest	person	interest	perhaps	underbrush	80
interest	interact	underpass	pepper	understand	underbrush	pepper	interpret	person	perhaps	90
understand	underpass	permit	interact	underbrush	pepper	interest	person	pepper	interpret	100

Word Fluency 3

	Correct	Errors
1st Try		
2nd Try		

#									
10	carve	horse	starve	nurse	serve	forgive	remorse	observe	purse
20	horse	forgive	carve	serve	starve	remorse	verse	nurse	observe
30	forgive	serve	observe	horse	carve	verse	starve	remorse	nurse
40	observe	horse	remorse	carve	purse	verse	nurse	starve	serve
50	serve	verse	forgive	starve	nurse	carve	horse	verse	observe
60	verse	starve	forgive	horse	purse	serve	nurse	remorse	carve
70	remorse	purse	horse	verse	carve	horse	serve	carve	observe
80	starve	nurse	serve	purse	remorse	observe	horse	carve	horse
90	forgive	verse	nurse	remorse	purse	observe	starve	carve	starve
100	purse	starve	carve	nurse	remorse	serve	observe	verse	forgive

	Correct	Errors
1st Try		
2nd Try		

10	way	new	say	day	little	say	way	day	may	
20	say	may	day	way	little	may	new	may	little	
30	day	little	way	new	say	new	little	new	way	
40	way	say	new	day	little	say	new	say	way	may
50	say	new	way	new	day	little	new	may	new	little
60	day	way	may	little	new	little	say	little	say	day
70	way	day	say	way	new	little	way	new	may	new
80	day	new	way	say	little	may	new	day	new	little
90	little	way	say	day	may	little	day	little	may	say
100	may	say	day	new	way	say	may	day	say	new

	Correct	Errors
1st Try		
2nd Try		

What do you do when you're bored? Some of us just 11
sit and think, while others pick up a pen. If you have 23
a pen, you might sketch. It feels natural, so almost 33
everybody likes to sketch. Sketching is a basic form 42
of art where lines can turn into shapes. Some shapes 52
are so abstract that you may not know what they are. 63
Other shapes can remind you of familiar things, and 72
you can turn them into objects. Your pad gets filled 82
with art. When you sketch, you're getting absorbed 90
in art. You're expressing yourself by making art. 98

The bell rings, and class begins. Everyone is sitting 107
at a desk, and some begin to take notes. You begin 118
to sketch, and your lines become art. Your name 127
becomes art. The sun comes up—on your paper—and 137
stars appear, too. But, what happens when it's time 146
for the test? Where are your notes? Notes will help 156
you pass the test, but sketches won't. It's hard to 166
sketch and take notes at the same time! 174

Meet Michael A. Cummings. He was born in Los 183
Angeles. Now he lives in a 100-year old brownstone 192
in Harlem. Since he was a child, he liked to draw 203
and paint. He always knew he wanted to be an artist. 214
Then one day, he made a banner. He said to himself, 225
I don't need pens and brushes. I can sew my art. He 237
expresses himself with a sewing machine. His canvas 245
is fabric. 247

What different things could you use to express 255
yourself in art? 258

Correct	Errors
1st Try	2nd Try

Fame was in store for Elisa Kleven. She made a — 10
name for herself. It began when she was a little girl. — 21
Common scraps fascinated her, so she used scraps to — 30
make art. Nutshells became beds. Caps from drinks — 38
became small baking pans. She loved to make little — 47
settings. Elisa's settings inspired her. She began to — 55
tell little tales. Her tales led to books for children. — 65
Next, Elisa's scraps became 3-D art in her books. — 74
Yarn made a horse's mane, and twine made a — 83
first-rate bird's nest. Bits of colored rags made — 91
a dozen different shapes. Elisa had discovered — 98
something. Common scraps can make fantastic art. — 105

The first form of art was cave art. Cave artists made — 116
lots of sketches inside caves. Caves protected the art. — 125
Wind didn't hurt it, and water didn't wash it off. The — 136
sun didn't fade it. A hundred tales are told in cave — 147
art. Cave art tells the tales of the lives of cave people. — 159
The cave dwellers hunted and fished. They sketched — 167
crude maps and made messages for each other. The — 176
art they made is still there. The messages they left — 186
us tell us much. From cave art, we learn history. We — 197
learn about the lives of some of the first humans. We — 208
learn something even more important. We learn that — 216
humans have always been engaged with making art. — 224

Word Fluency 1

Correct	Errors
1st Try	
2nd Try	

acorn	equip	diet	moment	secret	silent	music	poem	fever	detect	10
silent	music	acorn	poem	diet	equip	moment	secret	detect	fever	20
moment	equip	diet	acorn	music	poem	silent	fever	secret	detect	30
acorn	silent	fever	moment	equip	diet	detect	secret	poem	music	40
silent	secret	acorn	diet	moment	music	fever	detect	equip	poem	50
secret	equip	music	fever	detect	silent	moment	silent	acorn	diet	60
music	poem	secret	moment	silent	moment	diet	acorn	detect	fever	70
acorn	fever	equip	moment	detect	silent	diet	acorn	music	silent	80
secret	equip	moment	detect	silent	detect	silent	poem	poem	music	90
diet	moment	poem	fever	equip	music	silent	detect	secret	acorn	100

Correct	Errors
1st Try	
2nd Try	

Words										Count
tornado	tornado	undergo	tuxedo	menu	videos	heroes	zeroes	goes	ago	10
videos	heroes	tornado	zeroes	undergo	tornado	menu	ago	goes		20
tuxedo	tornado	undergo	tornado	heroes	zeroes	videos	goes	menu	ago	30
tornado	videos	goes	tuxedo	tornado	undergo	ago	menu	zeroes	heroes	40
videos	menu	tornado	undergo	tuxedo	heroes	goes	ago	tornado	zeroes	50
menu	tornado	heroes	goes	ago	videos	zeroes	tornado	undergo		60
heroes	zeroes	menu	tornado	videos	tuxedo	undergo	tornado	ago	goes	70
tornado	goes	tuxedo	ago	undergo	menu	zeroes	heroes	videos		80
menu	tornado	tuxedo	undergo	videos	ago	goes	tornado	zeroes	heroes	90
undergo	tuxedo	zeroes	goes	tornado	heroes	videos	ago	menu	tornado	100

Word Fluency 3

	Correct	Errors
1st Try		
2nd Try		

10	supersonic	superstar	prevent	preset	predict	menu	tuxedo	undergo	report	result
20	superstar	supersonic	menu	tuxedo	report	undergo	prevent	result	preset	predict
30	supersonic	menu	superstar	predict	prevent	preset	undergo	result	undergo	tuxedo
40	preset	prevent	menu	supersonic	undergo	report	superstar	tuxedo	superstar	result
50	prevent	report	supersonic	superstar	preset	tuxedo	undergo	superstar	menu	predict
60	undergo	result	prevent	tuxedo	predict	preset	result	prevent	report	menu
70	superstar	supersonic	report	undergo	tuxedo	supersonic	predict	tuxedo	supersonic	preset
80	predict	preset	prevent	menu	supersonic	undergo	report	predict	superstar	report
90	preset	prevent	report	supersonic	superstar	predict	preset	tuxedo	prevent	result
100	report	menu	supersonic	predict	preset	result	menu	superstar	prevent	tuxedo

Word Fluency 4

	Correct	Errors
1st Try		
2nd Try		

through	though	right	good	great	year	through	great	right	year	10
though	good	great	through	right	though	good	year	great	right	20
through	year	good	though	year	good	right	through	good	though	30
right	good	though	great	through	year	great	though	right	year	40
good	through	right	though	great	through	year	good	great	through	50
year	though	good	right	year	good	through	though	right	right	60
though	through	year	great	good	year	great	through	though	though	70
year	great	though	good	right	through	year	good	great	good	80
right	though	great	through	year	good	though	through	year	great	90
through	good	though	right	great	right	though	great	though	through	100

Passage Fluency 1

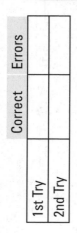

Errors	
Correct	
1st Try	2nd Try

They fill comic strips and have superhuman skills. 8
They're strong, quick, talented, and wise. They 15
ensure that good wins over evil. Who are these 24
superhumans? Superheroes! We all love heroes, as 31
heroes can inspire us and give us hope. 39

Humans wanted to make sense of their world. They 48
wanted to understand its order and its origin. They 57
strived to understand its conflicts, so they made up 66
tales to explain their world. These tales are called 75
myths. Myths are just made-up tales, but people 83
have believed them. People have lived their lives as 92
if myths were based in fact. In these tales, different 102
gods ruled over the world. 107

Long ago, the Romans told about the gods in their 117
myths. Saturn was one of their gods, the god of time. 128
Saturn had three sons: Jupiter, Neptune, and Pluto. 136
Jupiter ruled the air and was the king of the gods. He 148
was the strongest god. Juno was Jupiter's wife, and 157
the goddess of husbands and wives. Neptune ruled 165
the seas. He gave the waves white caps and made the 176
waters still. He held the fate of ships in his hands, 187
so a trip could be safe or unsafe. It was Neptune's 198
choice. His brother, Pluto, ruled over the dead. 206
His kingdom was a dark and gloomy land. Pluto 215
ruled over all who entered his kingdom. Once the 224
dead entered Pluto's underworld, they could never 231
leave. These myths are still told. Ancient myths are 240
intriguing. They give us insight into how the people 249
who lived before us explained what happened in the 258
world. 259

Correct	Errors
1st Try	
2nd Try	

Not every hero is a superhero. For some, spending 9
their lives helping others is a job. Think of 18
firefighters, soldiers, and police. Often, these are the 26
unsung heroes, as they risk their lives. 33

No matter where you live, fire can be a big problem. 44
Firefighters save lives when a home catches fire. A 53
call to 911 is a call to save lives. It's your direct line 66
to the unsung heroes. What happens when a forest 75
catches fire? Fires burn huge plots of land, and they 85
kill birds and plants. Enter the unsung heroes, as 94
they put out the fires. 99

When men and women join the military, they put 108
their lives on the line. They protect us and watch over 119
the homelands. Sometimes, war breaks out, so they 127
are called to protect and defend. No matter what the 137
issue, some people support it, and others reject it. 146
It is hard to do your job when many people do not 158
support you. Yet our soldiers do their jobs and expect 168
nothing in return. We should have pride in them. 177
They deserve their country's thanks. They, too, are 186
unsung heroes. 188

Crime is a big problem. Some people shoplift or use 198
drugs. Some are reckless drivers, and some harm 206
others. The police are there to help and bring back 216
order. They help solve crimes and work to make our 226
lives safer. Like soldiers and firefighters, they are 234
unsung heroes. 236

Word Fluency 1

	Correct	Errors
1st Try		
2nd Try		

became	beside	define	debate	finite	demote	migrate	locate	polite	describe	10
locate	migrate	became	demote	define	beside	debate	finite	describe	polite	20
debate	beside	define	became	migrate	locate	demote	polite	finite	describe	30
became	demote	polite	define	beside	finite	describe	finite	locate	migrate	40
locate	finite	define	debate	describe	migrate	polite	describe	beside	demote	50
finite	beside	polite	migrate	describe	demote	debate	locate	became	define	60
migrate	locate	became	describe	demote	debate	define	became	describe	polite	70
became	polite	beside	define	describe	finite	became	locate	migrate	demote	80
finite	beside	debate	locate	define	describe	polite	became	demote	migrate	90
define	debate	locate	polite	beside	migrate	demote	describe	finite	became	100

Correct	Errors
1st Try	
2nd Try	

athlete	complete	compute	admire	inside	include	provide	promote	presume	describe	10
promote	provide	athlete	include	compute	complete	admire	inside	describe	presume	20
admire	complete	compute	athlete	provide	promote	include	presume	inside	describe	30
athlete	include	presume	admire	complete	compute	describe	inside	promote	provide	40
promote	inside	athlete	compute	include	provide	presume	describe	complete	admire	50
inside	complete	provide	presume	describe	include	admire	promote	athlete	compute	60
provide	promote	inside	complete	include	admire	compute	athlete	describe	presume	70
athlete	presume	complete	include	describe	compute	inside	promote	provide	admire	80
inside	complete	admire	compute	promote	describe	presume	athlete	include	provide	90
compute	admire	promote	presume	complete	provide	include	describe	inside	athlete	100

Word Fluency 3

	Correct	Errors
1st Try		
2nd Try		

10	arrive	comprise	dispose	impose	passive	positive	primitive	repetitive	promise	purchase
20	repetitive	primitive	arrive	positive	dispose	comprise	impose	passive	purchase	promise
30	impose	comprise	dispose	arrive	primitive	repetitive	positive	promise	passive	purchase
40	arrive	positive	promise	impose	comprise	dispose	purchase	passive	repetitive	primitive
50	repetitive	passive	arrive	dispose	positive	primitive	promise	purchase	comprise	impose
60	passive	comprise	primitive	promise	purchase	positive	impose	repetitive	arrive	dispose
70	primitive	repetitive	passive	comprise	positive	impose	dispose	arrive	purchase	promise
80	arrive	promise	comprise	positive	purchase	dispose	passive	repetitive	primitive	impose
90	passive	comprise	impose	dispose	repetitive	purchase	promise	arrive	positive	primitive
100	dispose	impose	repetitive	promise	comprise	primitive	positive	purchase	passive	arrive

	Correct	Errors
1st Try		
2nd Try		

want	work	today	tomorrow	sound	again	today	sound	tomorrow	again	10
work	want	sound	today	again	want	tomorrow	work	want	tomorrow	20
again	sound	today	work	sound	work	again	tomorrow	today	want	30
today	tomorrow	again	sound	work	want	tomorrow	work	today	sound	40
again	want	tomorrow	today	again	sound	today	again	sound	again	50
want	today	tomorrow	again	sound	work	work	want	today	tomorrow	60
sound	want	again	tomorrow	today	work	work	again	tomorrow	want	70
work	today	sound	again	tomorrow	sound	work	again	tomorrow	today	80
today	sound	work	again	today	tomorrow	today	work	sound	tomorrow	90
again	want	tomorrow	today	work	sound	want	sound	tomorrow	work	100

Passage Fluency 1

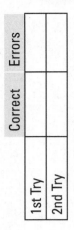

Correct | Errors

1st Try | 2nd Try

One person can make things happen, as Eunice	8
Kennedy Shriver did. She began a summer day camp	17
in 1963. She held the camp at her home and invited	28
athletes like Steven. She watched them compete in	36
sports and saw their desire to work hard and win.	46
She planned games such as swimming and track.	54
Competing was a thrill, and they loved it! They were	64
happy. Shriver saw them smile, and she made up her	74
mind. In 1968, her camp became Special Olympics,	82
and the games grew. More people came, and by 1970,	92
all 50 states sent athletes. Now, Special Olympics is	101
important in the lives of many people. Today, there	110
are 27 official sports, including summer sports and	118
winter sports. From all over the world, athletes come	127
to take part in the games. These athletes compete at	137
no cost. How are the games funded? Shriver has used	147
grants, and many have donated money. Many others	155
have made money by holding events. You can help,	164
too, so get started and help fund Special Olympics!	173

	Correct	Errors
1st Try		
2nd Try		

Some athletes love risks, so when they do their sport,   10
they add a twist. Extreme sports have added risks   19
that can give athletes a thrill. Skating is an example,   29
and extreme skaters are fine athletes. They take some   38
risks, and for them, it's fun.   44

Extreme skaters use in-line skates, which are not   52
like skates of the past. The skates are light, fast, and   63
strong. Skaters don't use skating rinks; they use skate   72
parks that have ramps. Skaters even have a jargon,   81
or their own words. Take the metal bar at the top of   93
the ramp where they do tricks. It has a name. It's the   105
"coping." The skaters twist, turn, and do amazing   113
jumps. They spend lots of time practicing. They start   122
with easy in-line tricks. First, there's the "crossover,"   130
where they just cross one skate over the other. Then   140
they practice harder tricks, but learning them takes   148
time. For example, they try "bashing," or going down   157
steps. Sometimes, there's no skate park, so they go   166
somewhere else. They use steps, parking lots, and   174
even curbs. They really take skating to the next level!   184

Extreme athletes protect themselves by using   190
helmets and pads, but they still can be injured.   199
Without protection, skaters can get hurt even more.   207
They can miss a landing or lose control. Extreme   216
athletes are risk-takers, and they love to compete   224
and take their sport to a new level. But they think   235
of safety, too. They have to. They have fun, but   245
they need to always take care. They need to be   255
safe athletes.   257

Word Fluency 1

	Correct	Errors
1st Try		
2nd Try		

10	why	sky	fly	imply	deny	rely	try	dry	by	my
20	sky	rely	why	by	dry	fly	my	imply	deny	try
30	why	dry	sky	try	imply	by	fly	rely	my	deny
40	fly	sky	by	why	rely	dry	deny	my	try	imply
50	by	why	dry	my	deny	sky	try	imply	fly	rely
60	dry	by	deny	why	my	imply	fly	rely	sky	try
70	my	deny	try	fly	dry	why	by	sky	rely	imply
80	rely	why	my	sky	imply	try	deny	fly	by	dry
90	deny	my	why	try	rely	sky	dry	imply	by	fly
100	why	rely	try	dry	deny	my	fly	by	sky	imply

Word Fluency 2

	Correct	Errors
1st Try		
2nd Try		

Words										#
happy	story	body	baby	thirty	tiny	army	penny	copy	candy	10
thirty	tiny	happy	army	story	copy	body	candy	baby	penny	20
happy	story	thirty	body	tiny	candy	copy	penny	army	baby	30
body	thirty	story	candy	happy	penny	army	baby	tiny	copy	40
happy	candy	army	penny	copy	baby	thirty	story	tiny	body	50
candy	penny	copy	body	happy	tiny	story	thirty	army	army	60
copy	happy	candy	baby	story	penny	story	army	body	tiny	70
body	story	army	copy	candy	happy	penny	candy	baby	thirty	80
army	happy	penny	thirty	story	tiny	body	copy	candy	baby	90
penny	copy	body	happy	army	thirty	baby	candy	tiny	story	100

Word Fluency 3

	Correct	Errors
1st Try		
2nd Try		

#									
10	pretty	quickly	bye	eye	system	type	gym	comply	supply
20	system	pretty	gym	eye	property	supply	quickly	bye	type
30	gym	quickly	property	type	pretty	comply	system	bye	eye
40	property	type	quickly	pretty	gym	bye	quickly	system	comply
50	pretty	quickly	system	supply	eye	type	bye	property	gym
60	system	pretty	eye	quickly	gym	comply	supply	property	type
70	pretty	quickly	comply	property	bye	gym	system	eye	supply
80	comply	pretty	type	bye	property	supply	bye	quickly	system
90	gym	bye	supply	property	system	property	pretty	eye	type
100	supply	pretty	bye	comply	quickly	type	property	system	eye

	Correct	Errors
1st Try		
2nd Try		

engine	certain	answer	poor	oil	laugh	answer	engine	poor	laugh	10
answer	engine	oil	certain	laugh	poor	certain	laugh	answer	engine	20
certain	laugh	poor	engine	oil	answer	oil	answer	engine	laugh	30
poor	oil	answer	laugh	certain	engine	poor	engine	laugh	certain	40
laugh	answer	answer	certain	engine	certain	laugh	laugh	poor	answer	50
answer	certain	engine	poor	poor	oil	poor	answer	engine	certain	60
engine	laugh	answer	laugh	oil	poor	answer	laugh	oil	engine	70
laugh	oil	engine	poor	certain	answer	poor	certain	answer	laugh	80
poor	laugh	answer	oil	engine	certain	laugh	engine	poor	answer	90
answer	oil	engine	certain	poor	oil	poor	laugh	engine	certain	100

Passage Fluency 1

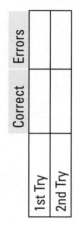

Errors   Correct

1st Try   2nd Try

Solve this puzzle: Its huge base is flat and has four 11
corners and four sides. The sides slope up, but the top 22
isn't flat. It has a sharp tip and was made long ago in 35
Egypt, where about 90 of them remain. You figured it 45
out. It's a pyramid, and it's amazing! 52

Pyramids were constructed for two basic uses. First, 60
they were sacred sites where rites were performed. 68
Second, they were designed as final resting sites, the 77
graves of kings. 80

The pyramids were constructed long ago, when there 88
were no motors. There were probably no cranes, and 97
workers may not have even had wheels. It seems like 107
an impossible task. The stones the workers moved 115
were huge, and they made millions of stone blocks. 124
One base block was so big, it weighed 70 tons. How 135
did they do it? Their method involved steps. First, they 145
dug the stone, and then it was put on a raft. The raft 158
drifted down the Nile River. At the site, the stone was 169
taken off, and workers chipped and shaped it. They 178
sculpted and carved a channel into the stone. Next, 187
they drove a wooden wedge into it. They drenched the 197
wedge in water, and it expanded. They added more 206
water, so the wedge expanded more. At last, the stone 216
split, and they cut it. They used chisels and stone 226
hammers to make it the desired shape. Up the ramps it 237
went, and the pyramid rose. So did the ramps. Stones 247
were dragged into place as block stacked upon block. 256
Finally, the workers reached the top where they put 265
on a capstone, and it was finished. One more amazing 275
pyramid! 276

	Correct	Errors
1st Try		
2nd Try		

Visualize yourself living in a different place and | 8
time—how about ancient Egypt? What would be | 16
different about your life and what would be the same | 26
as your life now? Let's travel back in time where we'll | 37
meet two young people living in ancient Egypt. | 45

First, meet Moses, a farmer's son. In Egypt, people | 54
depend on farmers because they supply all the | 62
crops. During the growing season from November | 69
to February, Moses helps his dad plant the crops. | 78
They work to plow the rich, black soil that has been | 89
brought by the Nile. They work to make certain the | 99
crops will be plentiful. By June, the crops need to | 109
be harvested and stored. Moses' dad cannot farm | 117
the land from June to September because the Nile | 126
River floods in these months. It floods their fields | 135
and brings new, rich soil to cover the land. When the | 146
river floods, they work elsewhere. Moses and his dad | 155
work on the pyramids. When the river subsides, they | 164
return home, and life on the farm begins again. | 173

Hebeny studies hard because she wants to be a | 182
scribe. She studies at home because only boys can go | 192
to school. Her father is a scribe, and his job is highly | 204
valued in Egypt. It is one of the few jobs that requires | 216
a formal education. The writing is done with a code. | 226
The code doesn't have letters as we know them. It | 236
uses symbols to represent ideas. Most scribes are | 244
men, but Hebeny wants to master the skill. She wants | 254
to work as a scribe like her dad. | 262

Word Fluency 1

	Correct	Errors
1st Try		
2nd Try		

#										
10	why	direct	diet	report	remote	line	try	alone	short	sharp
20	direct	line	why	short	alone	diet	sharp	report	remote	try
30	why	alone	direct	try	report	short	diet	remote	sharp	line
40	diet	direct	short	why	remote	alone	try	sharp	diet	report
50	short	why	alone	sharp	line	direct	diet	line	direct	remote
60	alone	short	remote	why	sharp	report	why	report	line	try
70	sharp	line	try	diet	report	why	short	direct	remote	report
80	remote	why	sharp	direct	report	remote	try	report	alone	short
90	line	sharp	why	try	direct	alone	line	direct	report	diet
100	why	remote	try	alone	line	sharp	diet	short	report	direct

Word Fluency 2

	Correct	Errors
1st Try		
2nd Try		

sunrise	sunset	something	sometimes	transport	translate	prevent	pretend	contact	contest	10
transport	translate	sunrise	prevent	sunset	contact	sometimes	contest	something	pretend	20
sunrise	sunset	transport	sometimes	translate	contest	contact	pretend	prevent	something	30
sometimes	transport	sunset	contest	sunrise	pretend	prevent	something	translate	contact	40
sunrise	contest	prevent	pretend	contact	something	transport	translate	sunset	sometimes	50
contest	pretend	prevent	contact	contest	sometimes	something	sunset	translate	prevent	60
contact	pretend	contact	something	contest	contest	transport	prevent	sunset	translate	70
sometimes	sunset	sunrise	prevent	contact	sunrise	prevent	translate	something	transport	80
prevent	sunrise	pretend	sunrise	transport	pretend	sometimes	contact	contest	something	90
pretend	contact	sometimes	sunrise	prevent	sometimes	contest	something	contest	sunset	100

Word Fluency 3

	Correct	Errors
1st Try		
2nd Try		

Line	Words									
10	again	certain	gone	laugh	poor	they	bye	though	today	tomorrow
20	laugh	bye	though	again	today	certain	they	gone	tomorrow	poor
30	they	again	bye	poor	certain	tomorrow	laugh	today	though	gone
40	certain	poor	they	though	again	bye	gone	tomorrow	laugh	today
50	gone	today	certain	laugh	laugh	they	again	poor	though	tomorrow
60	laugh	bye	again	today	gone	certain	though	they	tomorrow	poor
70	again	they	poor	laugh	bye	gone	today	certain	though	tomorrow
80	poor	gone	though	they	today	again	bye	laugh	tomorrow	certain
90	laugh	though	they	certain	tomorrow	poor	today	again	bye	gone
100	they	poor	gone	today	laugh	though	certain	bye	tomorrow	again

Word Fluency 4

	Correct	Errors
1st Try		
2nd Try		

10	who	want	what	answer	people	there	their	two	too	to
20	there	who	two	people	too	want	to	what	answer	their
30	two	what	want	their	who	too	there	answer	to	people
40	want	their	who	two	answer	to	what	people	to	too
50	who	what	there	who	people	their	two	want	to	two
60	there	who	people	to	what	too	want	two	answer	their
70	who	what	want	answer	two	two	answer	their	people	to
80	too	who	their	to	want	to	people	want	what	there
90	two	answer	to	there	there	who	want	people	what	their
100	to	who	answer	what	their	what	two	two	there	people

Passage Fluency 1

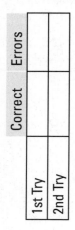

	Errors
Correct	
1st Try	2nd Try

The temperature is below zero, and the wind gusts | 9
at more than 200 mph! The wind chill hits the | 19
danger zone, and the land is frozen. Welcome to the | 29
continent of Antarctica, home of the South Pole. It | 38
is very dry and cold, yet life can still be found. Small | 50
plants live on the frozen shore, and krill thrive in the | 61
cold waters. Whales migrate to Antarctica just for | 69
krill. Other forms of life, such as seals and penguins, | 79
visit too. | 81

In Antarctica, days are far from what we think of as | 92
normal. In the summer, there is constant day, and it | 102
is never dark. Summer begins in October and ends | 111
in March, the fall and winter months in the U.S. | 121
When the southern hemisphere tilts toward the | 128
sun, Antarctica has constant sunshine. Is it hard to | 137
go to bed when the sun is still up, so dwellings in | 149
Antarctica have thick shades to make it dark inside. | 158

When the southern hemisphere tilts away from the | 166
sun, it is winter in Antarctica. Then, it is dark all the | 178
time. It's hard to get up in the dark. An alarm clock | 190
wakes you; not the rising sun. There is some light in | 201
the sky that comes from gases. Swirling gases color | 210
the winter sky. To adjust to the constant darkness | 219
takes time! | 221

People do not make the Antarctic their home, so they | 231
come for a short time. They study, write, and uncover | 241
secrets from the past that unlock the future. | 249

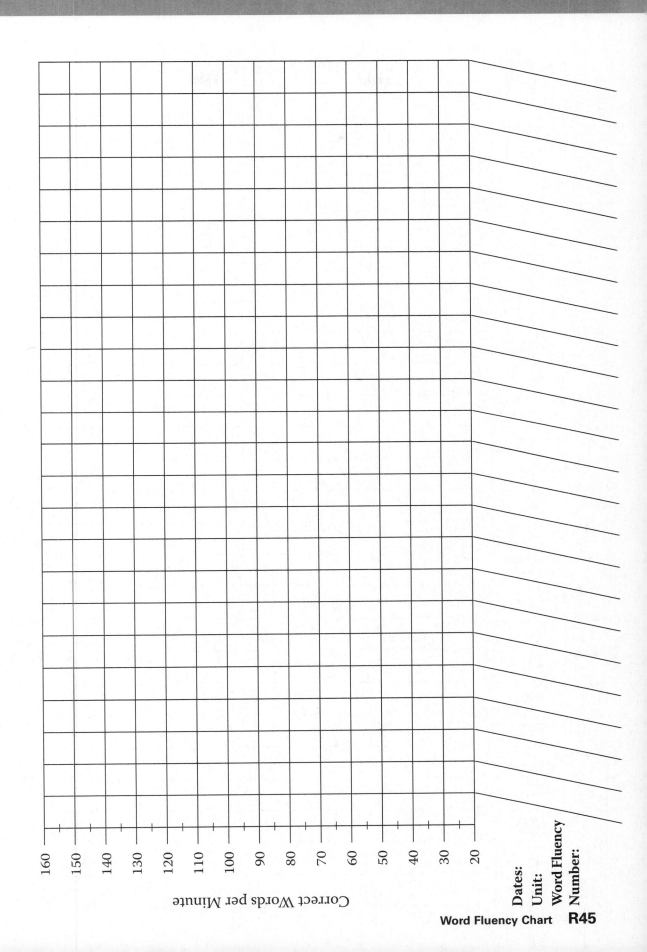

Word Fluency Chart

Correct Words per Minute

160
150
140
130
120
110
100
90
80
70
60
50
40
30
20

Dates:
Unit:
Word Fluency
Number:

Word Fluency Chart **R45**

Fluency Charts

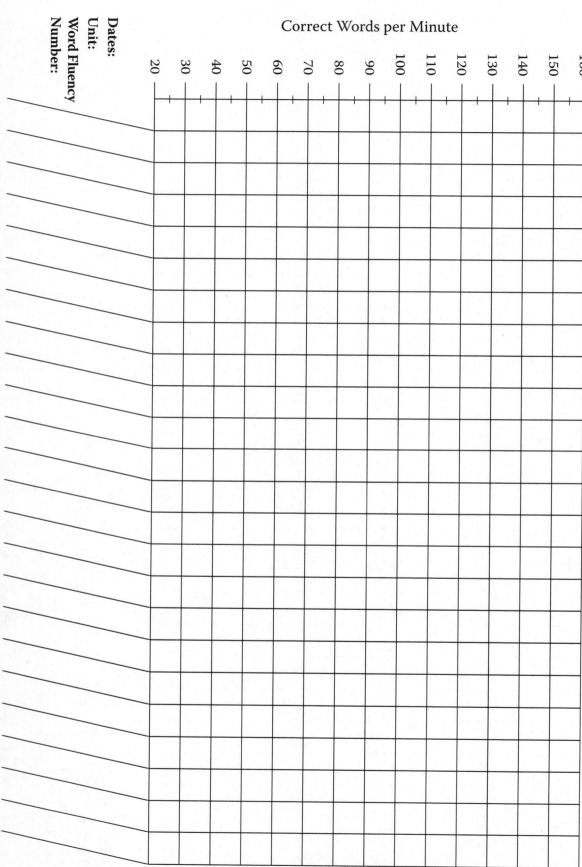

Correct Words per Minute

20　30　40　50　60　70　80　90　100　110　120　130　140　150　160

Dates:
Unit:
Word Fluency
Number:

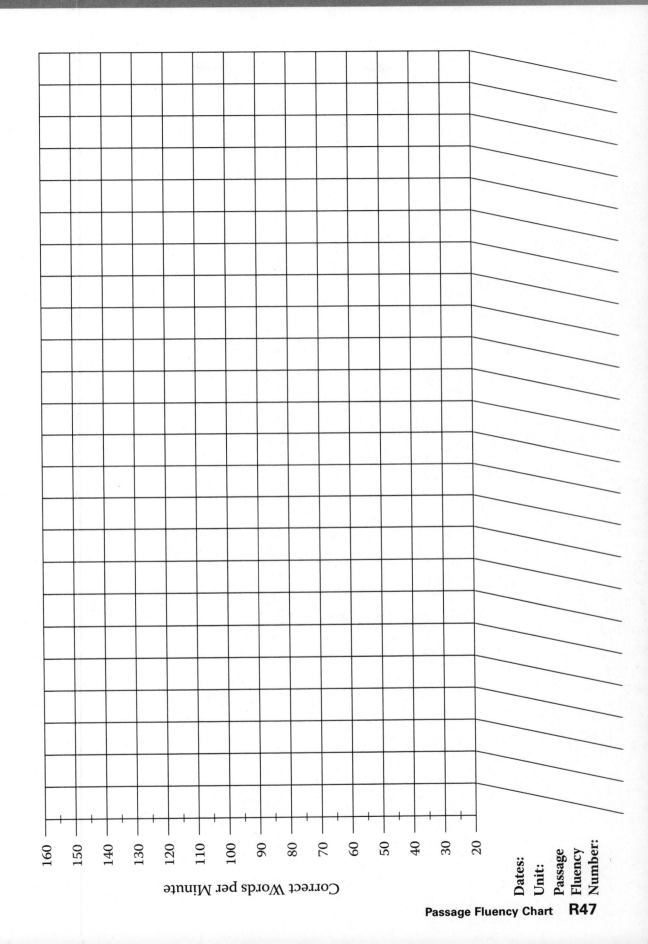

Passage Fluency Chart

Correct Words per Minute

160 150 140 130 120 110 100 90 80 70 60 50 40 30 20

Dates:

Unit:

Passage
Fluency
Number:

Essential Word Cards

Unit 13

gone	look	most
people	see	water

Unit 14

day	little	may
new	say	way

Essential Word Cards

Unit 15

good	great	right
though	through	year

Unit 16

again	sound	today
tomorrow	want	work

Essential Word Cards

Unit 17

answer	certain	engine
laugh	oil	poor

Word Building Letter Cards

a	a	b	b	c	c	d
d	f	f	g	g	h	h
i	i	j	j	k	k	l
l	m	m	n	n	o	o
p	p	qu	qu	r	r	s
s	t	t	v	v	w	w
x	x	y	y	z	z	ck
ck	ll	ll	ss	ss	ff	ff
zz	zz	ar	er	ir	or	ur

Word Building Letter Cards

D	C	C	B	B	A	A
H	H	G	G	F	F	D
L	K	K	J	J	I	I
O	O	N	N	M	M	L
S	R	R	Qu	Qu	P	P
W	W	V	V	T	T	S
	Z	Z	Y	Y	X	X

Student _____ Date _____

Syllable Types

Bank It

Student _____ Date _____

Prefixes

Bank It

Student _____ Date_____

Prefixes

Bank It

Student _____ Date _____

Suffixes
